Because of Jane

By Shannon Brown

Because of Jane
© 2025 Shannon Brown
All rights reserved.

For permission requests, please contact:
Shannon Brown

becauseofjanenovel@gmail.com

First eBook Edition — 2025
Published in the United States of America

Dedication

For my mom,
 my hero, my heart, and my greatest teacher.

You are the woman who showed me what strength truly looks like.
 From you, I learned how to stand tall, to keep fighting, and to face life's hardest moments with grace and courage.

Even when you didn't always agree with my choices, your love never wavered. You've given me a lifetime of strength, compassion, and the belief that I could survive anything.

Thank you for being the best mom you could be, and for showing me how to be a warrior.

Prologue

When the box opened again, for the first time in what felt like an eternity, I looked up into a woman's face that I thought I recognized. The blue eyes were the same, and the long blonde hair fell in familiar waves around her shoulders, but this was no longer the young woman I once knew. Her features were older, softer yet wiser, touched by the weight of years that had passed without me.

"Hello, Jane," the woman said, her voice warm and steady as she smiled down at me. She reached forward, running her fingers gently through my hair as if no time had passed at all. "It's been a long time, and you haven't changed a bit."

The moment her touch brushed my cheek, I knew it was her. Maddie. My Maddie. My companion from another lifetime. But now she stood before me as a woman, no longer the child who once confided in me, laughed with me, and cried into my arms. No longer the teenager who always kept me at her side. Her belly was round, glowing with new life, and only then did I notice where I was: a nursery. Soft light filtered through gauzy curtains, and the faint scent of baby powder and lavender drifted through the air.

Maddie guided my hands forward until I was reaching for her, and without hesitation, she pulled me into her embrace. The warmth of it flooded through me, familiar and comforting, like stepping back into a memory I thought had been lost forever. For a heartbeat, the years melted away.

"It's time for you to take care of another little one," Maddie whispered against me, her words laced with affection and trust. "I don't know what I would have done without you when I was growing up. You helped me through some of the hardest times in my life, Jane. Times when I felt lost, when I didn't know how to go on, you were always there. You never left me."

And in that moment, the memory surged back. I could almost hear it again, the sharp rise of her dad's voice echoing from the living room, the crash of something breaking, and the muffled sobs of her mother. Maddie had stood frozen at the top of the darkened staircase, the lights off, clutching me tightly against her chest. Her small body trembled as each shout and thud below made her flinch, but she buried her face into me, drawing strength from the silence I offered. I had been the only shield she had, the one place she could hide when the world downstairs felt too frightening to face.

Her voice now broke through the memory, softer than before, carrying a weight that only she and I could ever truly understand. She placed me carefully onto a soft blue rocking chair positioned beside the crib, her hands lingering for just a moment before she turned toward the door. With a final, almost reverent look, she walked out, leaving me alone in this new chapter of her story.

I hopped down and padded across the room, taking it all in. This was not the house I remembered, but Maddie's essence was everywhere. Her tastes hadn't changed. Her love for Disney shone through every detail. The walls were alive with color, painted murals of Winnie the Pooh and his friends. Each brushstroke brimming with whimsy and tenderness. A shelf of plush toys stood ready, and the crib itself was draped with soft linens embroidered with honeybees and balloons.

The air felt heavy with both nostalgia and anticipation. Maddie had grown, but she had brought me with her into this new life, just as she once had when she was small. And now, it seemed, my purpose was beginning again.

Chapter One

The story begins one winter evening, long before the nursery, long before Maddie grew into the woman I had just seen.

It was Christmas. Not the bustling kind you see in movies, with crowded houses, family laughter, and overflowing stockings. No, this Christmas was quiet, almost too quiet. The tree was small, tucked into the corner of the living room. Its branches strung with mismatched ornaments and colored lights that blinked with a faint, uneven hum. The air smelled faintly of pine and cinnamon, though it couldn't mask the lingering emptiness of a missing presence.

Maddie's father wasn't there. He was off drinking with his friends and cousins, as he so often was, leaving behind an ache that Maddie was too young to name but old enough to feel. She sat cross-legged on the carpet in her little mermaid pajamas, her little hands resting in her lap as she watched the twinkling lights and the snow falling through the large picture window.

Wyatt, her older brother, was nearby, building towers out of his new wooden blocks. He made sound effects, explosions and crashes, as each one toppled to the floor. Every so often, he glanced at Maddie, teasing her to come play, but she stayed close to her papa, waiting, as if she knew something special was about to happen.

In the background, a record player spun Raffi's Christmas Album. His gentle voice filled the room with "Frosty the Snowman," soft and cheerful against the quiet of the night. The music gave the small living room a warmth that even the blinking lights alone couldn't provide. Maddie loved this album. Her favorite song that she liked to listen to on repeat was "Old Toy Trains."

Her papa, her grandfather, was one of her favorite people. He noticed the way Maddie's smile didn't quite reach her eyes. Kneeling beside her, he handed her a box wrapped in silver paper, a gold ribbon tied neatly around it.

"This one's for you, Maddie-girl," he said with a twinkle in his eye, his salt and pepper beard trimmed neatly, but reminded Maddie a little of Santa Claus.

Her eyes widened. "For me? Really, Papa? It's so shiny! Did you wrap it all by yourself?" She asked, looking at him skeptically.

He chuckled. "I might've had a little help with the ribbon. But what's inside, that's all me." He said putting his hands up in the air playfully.

Maddie tore the paper with quick, eager hands, squealing when the gold ribbon came free. Wyatt stopped his play to watch, his blocks forgotten as Maddie lifted the lid.

Inside, I was waiting. I will never forget the first time I saw Maddie's face.

Maddie gasped so loudly her mother poked her head in from the kitchen to see all the excitement. "Ohhh! Papa, look at her dress! It's pink! And it's got little lacy ruffles!" She smoothed my tiny skirt with her fingertips, her blue eyes wide with wonder. "She's the prettiest doll I've ever seen!"

Her papa smiled, watching her hug me to her chest. "Every little girl needs a friend she can always count on. Someone who will listen. Someone who won't ever leave her side."

Maddie giggled, bouncing slightly as she pressed her cheek against my bonnet. "Can I keep her forever, Papa? I'll take real good care of her. I promise, cross my heart."

"Of course," Papa said gently. "She's all yours. Her name is Jane." he said passing Maddie my birth certificate from the box.

"Jane," Maddie repeated, her voice soft with awe. She tilted her head as if listening to me. "Hi, Jane. Don't worry, I'll be your best friend."

Wyatt leaned closer, squinting at me. "She looks fancy," he muttered, poking at my bonnet before turning back to his blocks. "Just don't let her boss you around."

Maddie stuck her tongue out at him before hugging me tighter. "She won't. She's nice. She's mine."

"I was talking to her," Wyatt teased, pointing to Jane playfully. Maddie stuck out her tongue at him.

From that Christmas night on, I was more than just a doll. I was Maddie's friend, her confidante, the one she whispered secrets to in the dark when no one else was listening. In a house where voices sometimes rose and shadows loomed, I was the one constant she could always hold tight.

And in her papa's gift, Maddie had found not just a toy, but the companion she needed most.

Chapter Two

That night, after the last of the wrapping paper had been gathered and Raffi's voice had faded to silence, Maddie carried me carefully into her room. She held me close against her chest as though I might slip away if she loosened her grip.

Her room was small, tucked on the second floor of the old house, where the heat from the wood stove downstairs rarely reached. The stove crackled faintly below, its warmth strong enough to keep the living room cozy but thin by the time it drifted upstairs to Maddie and Wyatt's rooms. Maddie's breath puffed in little clouds when she first climbed beneath the covers at night, though she was used to it.

The walls of her room were plain white, with faint scuffs and fingerprints that told stories of years of play. A single twin bed sat against the wall, covered in a quilt her mama had made long ago, its fabric patches soft from use. A small dresser leaned slightly on uneven legs in the corner, and the flowered curtains swayed whenever a draft snuck through the old window frame.

Wyatt's laughter could still be heard faintly down the hall as he played with his blocks, but Maddie's world had narrowed to me alone.

She set me gently on her bed, smoothing out my pink, lacy dress as if I were a real person. She sat cross-legged across from me, her hair falling loose over her shoulders, her blue eyes locked on mine.

"Hi, Jane," she whispered, almost shyly. "Papa said that's your name, and I think it's a good one. You're my doll now. That means you're my best friend, and I am your best friend too."

Then, as though remembering her manners, Maddie gasped softly. "Oh! You have to meet my other friends and your new roommates. It wouldn't be fair if I didn't introduce you."

She carried me to the chair in the corner where a worn stuffed bunny sat waiting, its fur thinned and one ear flopped lower than the other. Maddie straightened her shoulders, cleared her throat, and said in her most "grown-up" voice:

"Rabberta, I would like you to meet Jane. Jane, this is Rabberta. Grammy gave her to me when I was just a baby, so she's basically the boss around here." She lowered me so that my face nearly touched the bunny's. "Rabberta, please be nice. Jane's new and she's shy. She has a very pretty pink dress, see? And lace! You'll like her."

Then she moved us to the little wooden crib by the dresser, where another doll was tucked in carefully under a faded Rainbow Bright blanket. Maddie crouched down and whispered, "And this is Trisha. She's my first baby doll. But shhh, she's asleep right now. Trisha gets cranky if she doesn't get her nap. You can talk to her tomorrow when she's up."

Maddie plopped back down on the bed with me in her arms, looking proud of herself. "There. Now everybody knows everybody. You're part of the family, Jane." She hugged me tight, her small face pressing against my bonnet. "Don't worry. I'll always take care of you. You'll never be lonely."

Her eyelids drooped, heavy with sleep, but her voice carried the weight of a promise. "I'll tell you everything, Jane. Everything."

The room fell quiet except for the creak of the house settling and the faint pop of the wood stove downstairs. And so began the very first night of Maddie's secrets, her dreams, and her heart, shared with me.

Chapter Three

It was sometime after midnight when the crash came. The sound of glass shattering against the floor jolted Maddie awake. She sat up in her little twin bed, her quilt falling into her lap, her heart pounding as shouts echoed up from the living room below.

She clutched me to her chest, her small fingers digging into my pink, lacy dress as if she could squeeze the fear away. "Jane," she whispered in the dark, her breath trembling, "something's wrong."

Another voice rose, her father's, rough and angry. Then her mother's voice, sharp and tired, yelling back. The words tumbled over each other, too fast and loud to make sense, but the tone was enough to send a shiver through Maddie's small frame.

She slipped out of bed, her bare feet cold against the floorboards. The hallway creaked as she tiptoed toward the stairs, holding me so close my bonnet brushed against her chin. She sat at the very top step, knees pulled to her chest, listening to the storm below.

Wyatt's door opened with a groan, and he stepped into the hall rubbing his eyes. His hair stuck up at odd angles, and he looked older than his eight years in the pale glow of the hallway light.

"Maddie?" he whispered. "What's happening?"

Maddie hugged me tighter, her voice thin and shaky. "They're fighting again. I think Daddy broke something."

Wyatt frowned, stepping closer. "We should stay up here. Don't go down there."

"I'm not," Maddie whispered back, her chin trembling. "I just... I need to hear Papa. He'll stop it."

"You always say that," Wyatt muttered, though he sank down beside her, his shoulder brushing hers. Together, they peered through the railing into the darkness below.

The yelling grew louder, her father's voice cutting through the house like thunder. Then came Papa's voice. It was steady, deep, and commanding. He didn't yell. He never yelled. But there was power in the way he spoke, enough to cut through the chaos.

"That's enough," Papa said firmly. "The children are sleeping. This ends now."

Her father barked back, voice rising in protest. "Don't tell me what to do in my own—"

"Sit down, and shut your mouth," Papa snapped, steel in his tone. He didn't have to shout; the weight of authority carried in every word. "You forget who you're talking to. Don't make me remind you."

The house went quiet. Everyone knew Papa had once been a police officer, and even though he had long since retired. He was someone her father feared. Not because of his size, though Papa was broad and strong, but because his presence left no room for defiance. He showed Maddie's dad no fear.

Her father's grumbling faded into silence. Her mother's voice dropped low, still tight with frustration but no longer sharp. Only Papa's footsteps carried through the room now, slow and measured, like a guard making sure the night stayed safe.

Maddie buried her face against me, whispering into my bonnet. "See, Jane? I told you. Papa always makes it better."

Wyatt glanced at her, his face pale in the dim light. "I hate when they fight. It makes my stomach hurt."

"Me too," Maddie admitted softly, rocking me back and forth. "But we've got Papa here right now. And I've got Jane now, too. And we've always got each other."

Wyatt didn't answer right away, but after a long pause, he sighed and leaned against her. "Just don't tell anybody I sat here with you, okay?"

Maddie almost smiled. "I won't. It'll be our secret."

At last, Papa's voice floated gently upward. "Back to bed, little ones. Everything's alright now."

Maddie obeyed, clutching me all the way back to her room, where she pulled the quilt over both of us and whispered into the dark, "I'll never let you go, Jane. You make me brave."

As she drifted off, I lay tucked in her arms, my bonnet warm against her cheek. Though I could not speak aloud, something had shifted inside me.

That night had taught me something: I was not just here to be held or dressed in lace. My purpose was greater.

When Maddie's heartbeat slowed against me, when her tears stayed unshed because she believed I was listening, I understood. I was not cloth and stitches. I was comfort. I was safety. I was her secret guard against the shadows of the house.

I was Jane.
I was Maddie's shield.
And no matter what storms raged around her, I would not leave her side.

Chapter Four

The house had finally grown still. Maddie's soft breathing rose and fell beneath the quilt, her arms curled protectively around where I had been. But once her grip loosened in sleep, I slipped free. My little cloth feet touched the wooden floorboards without a sound.

Moonlight spilled through the window in pale stripes, making the little room glow faintly. I padded toward the chair in the corner, where Rabberta sat slumped, her stitched paws resting in her lap.

Rabberta was a pink bunny, faded now from years of love, but still carrying the soft blush that had once made Maddie's eyes sparkle when she first held her. One ear stood tall, while the other flopped sideways, permanently bent from so many nights of being hugged too tightly. Around her neck was a satin ribbon, also pink, though fraying at the edges. Maddie had loved her immediately, because pink was her favorite color, and Grammy had known it when she chose the bunny years ago.

Rabberta stirred as if she had been waiting for me. Her button eyes glimmered in the moonlight.
"So," she said, her voice gentle but worn, "you're the new one."

I smoothed the ruffles of my pink, lacy dress. "I'm Jane. Papa gave me to her tonight, It's something called Christmas."

From the wooden crib near the dresser came a small rustle. Trisha, Maddie's first baby doll, opened her painted eyes. Her blanket slid down as she sat up stiffly, her porcelain cheeks catching the light. "So it's true. Maddie finally got a new friend."

I nodded. "She held me so tight tonight. I've never felt anything like it."

Rabberta tilted her head, her long ear drooping across her face. "She's been waiting for someone like you. Maddie's got a heart that shines brighter than she knows, but it's been bruised too many times. She needs you to help carry it."

I stepped closer, curious. "What do you mean?"

Trisha's painted lips curved into the smallest of smiles. "She's lonely, Jane. Her mama works too much. Her daddy... well, he's hardly here. Sometimes when he is, she wishes he wasn't. So Maddie makes her own world with us. She practices love and kindness in ways she doesn't always get back."

Rabberta gave a soft chuckle, though it held no real humor. "This ear" she tugged at the floppy one, "has soaked up more tears than I could ever count. Nights when she was scared, nights when the yelling downstairs wouldn't stop. She pressed her face into me until the storm passed."

I looked between them, my stitches tight with something like awe. "And now I'm here. But why me?"

Rabberta leaned forward, her faded pink fur glowing softly in the moonlight. "Because you're new and bright, untouched by the weight we've carried. Maddie believes you're strong. And what Maddie believes... that's what becomes true. Children give life to us."

"She'll tell you things she doesn't tell anyone else," Trisha added, folding her tiny arms like a little mother. "She'll whisper her secrets to you. That's your gift. And when the nights are dark, when fear presses in" her eyes flicked to the window as the wind rattled the panes, "you'll have to make her brave."

I turned back toward the bed, where Maddie slept with her hand stretched across the pillow where I had been. Her lips curled in the faintest smile, even in her dreams. She had welcomed me without hesitation.

"I'll do it," I said firmly. "I'll be what she needs. I'll never leave her."

Rabberta straightened, pride flickering in her button eyes. "Then welcome, Jane. You're part of the family now."

Trisha yawned delicately, lying back in her crib. "Get used to long nights. Maddie's life isn't an easy one, but it's worth every stitch of you."

The three of us fell silent as Maddie shifted in her sleep, pulling the quilt closer. Outside, the wind whispered against the old house, but inside her room there was a sense of peace.

I looked at them both, Rabberta the steady listener, Trisha the quiet caretaker, and I understood. I was not just another toy. I was the missing piece in Maddie's circle of guardians.

Chapter Five

The morning light slipped through the thin flowered curtains, brushing the little room with soft gold. Maddie stirred, rubbing her eyes and stretching beneath her quilt. Then, all at once, her nose twitched and she sat up straighter, sniffing the air.

"Bacon!" she whispered, her face breaking into a grin. She hopped from bed and pressed her forehead to the cool windowpane, breathing in deep. The coolness of the window made the smell intensify "And pancakes too! That means Papa's cooking."

When Papa was here, they ate well. He always said a good breakfast made you strong, and he never let the day begin without it.

Maddie turned back to her little world. She hugged me tight, then scooped up Rabberta from the chair and leaned over to kiss Trisha where she lay in her crib. "Morning, everybody," she whispered cheerfully.

She set us neatly back in our places, then padded to the small dresser against the wall. Its drawers stuck a little, but she tugged one open with determination. She rummaged through until she found her favorite dress: a second-hand pink one with tiny flowers scattered across the fabric. The color had faded in places, and a button near the top was loose, but Maddie adored it.

She slipped it on over her head, humming as she moved. The tune was soft but certain, the words slipping through her lips in little whispers: "The sun'll come out, tomorrow..." She swayed a little as she sang, her voice thin but filled with hope. Annie was her favorite musical, and that song made her believe, no matter how hard the

23

day before had been, that better days were always waiting.

Standing before the cracked mirror on her dresser, she picked up a little brush and carefully pulled her blonde hair into two neat braids. Most children her age still had their mothers fix their hair, but Maddie had learned to do it herself. Her hands were small and clumsy, but she had practiced so many times that now the braids held firm.

I watched her proudly, admiring her independence, until something caught my eye. As she leaned forward to adjust the hem of her dress, the fabric shifted. For just a moment, I saw the faint purplish shadows on her lower back.

Bruises.

The sight tightened something inside me. They did not belong on Maddie's small frame. She didn't notice me watching; she only tugged her dress down quickly, as if hiding them was second nature.

Then she twirled in front of the mirror, her skirt fluttering, her braids swinging. She turned toward us, her little eyes shining. "How do I look, Rabberta? Trisha? Jane?" she asked hopefully, giving a small curtsy.

The toys were silent, but I could feel what they would have said. Beautiful. Brave. Stronger than you know.

Maddie smiled, taking our silence as agreement. "I knew you'd think so."

She straightened, clutching me close again. "Let's go, Jane. Papa made breakfast."

And though she bounded happily toward the smell of bacon and pancakes, still humming the promise of Annie's song, I held the image of the bruises inside me. It was a secret I couldn't speak, but one I would never forget. Another reminder of why I was here, why I had to stay strong.

Because Maddie needed me.

Chapter Six

Maddie skipped down the narrow stairs, clutching me tight in one arm, her pink dress swishing at her knees. The smell of bacon and pancakes grew stronger with every step, and by the time she reached the bottom, her stomach gave a happy growl.

The kitchen was warm and glowing, the old gas stove humming with life. Papa stood in front of it, his broad back turned as he poured batter into the skillet. He tilted the pan with practiced precision, shaping the pancakes into circles big and small. A strip of bacon crackled beside them, filling the room with its rich, smoky scent.

At the table, Maddie's mom sat with her hair wrapped in a towel, still damp from her shower. A steaming mug of coffee rested in her hands, and she stared down into it as if the dark liquid might give her more strength than she had. Her bathrobe hung loosely around her shoulders, the belt tied in a half-hearted knot.

The kitchen smelled like heaven, pancakes and bacon, butter and syrup. The stove had warmed the whole room until it felt like a safe little cocoon against the winter chill outside.

"Good morning, Maddie-girl," Papa said with a smile as he turned, spatula in hand. His eyes softened when he saw her hugging me close. "You clean up real nice. That pink dress suits you."

Maddie twirled once, her braids bouncing. "Thank you, Papa!" she said proudly. She looked down at me and whispered, "Jane helped me pick it."

Papa chuckled and gave a little nod toward me. "Smart doll."

Just then, Wyatt shuffled into the kitchen in his blue pajamas that had the slippers attached, rubbing his eyes. His hair stuck up in wild tufts. "Smells good, Papa," he mumbled as he climbed into a chair at the table.

Papa turned back to the skillet. "Now hold on, you two. Got something special for breakfast today." He flipped a pancake with a flourish, then arranged two smaller ones as ears. With care, he dotted the top circle with two chocolate chips, making eyes that melted into place as the heat kissed them.

"Mickey!" Maddie squealed as he slid the pancake onto her plate. "Papa, it's perfect!"

Wyatt leaned forward, grinning despite the sleep still on his face. "Can I have one too?"

"Of course," Papa said with a wink, already pouring the next set of circles. "Nobody eats plain pancakes when I'm cooking. Life's too short for that."

Maddie's mom sighed and sipped her coffee, saying nothing, her towel slipping slightly as she adjusted it. The tired lines around her eyes softened just a little in the warmth of the kitchen, though her shoulders stayed slumped.

Papa crouched to Maddie's level as he set down her plate. "Eat up, sweetheart. Pancakes make the day brighter."

Maddie giggled and placed me gently on the table beside her plate. "Jane's eating too," she announced, carefully cutting a tiny piece of pancake and setting it near me.

Papa winked. "Then I'd better make sure Jane gets her share of Mickey too."

The little bubble of peace lasted until the sound of heavy footsteps echoed down the hallway. Maddie froze, fork halfway to her mouth. A moment later, her father stumbled into the kitchen.

His eyes were bloodshot, with huge bags beneath them, his skin pale and gray. The stench of stale beer, Budweiser, clung to him. He scratched at his unshaven jaw, muttering as he collapsed into a chair.

Papa's jaw tightened, though his voice stayed calm. "Coffee's on the counter," he said, not turning away from the stove.

The man's gaze shifted to Maddie's mom, who was quietly eating her breakfast. His lip curled. "You heard him," he barked. "Get my coffee ready."

Her fork hovered in midair, then slowly lowered to the plate. She started to rise from her chair, resignation written in every small movement, until Papa spoke again, his voice sharper now.

"She is eating," Papa said firmly, without looking up from the stove. "If you have legs, get it yourself."

The room went still. Wyatt stared down at his plate, quietly eating his pancakes. Maddie instinctively slid closer to me, pressing her fingers against my bonnet.

The sour heaviness of her father's presence hung in the air, pressing down on the warm bubble of safety Papa had built.

Her father glared, muttering under his breath, then shoved his chair back and stomped toward the counter. He grabbed the coffee pot with an irritated grunt and started to pour into his mug, but he wasn't paying attention. The coffee spilled over the rim and splashed across his hand.

"Dammit!" he roared, jerking back as the scalding liquid hit his skin. In a surge of rage, he hurled the coffee pot across the room.

It exploded against the cabinet with a violent crash. Shards of glass scattered across the kitchen floor, and a wave of steaming coffee sprayed in every direction. Maddie screamed as some of it splattered across her shoulder, soaking through her pink dress and searing the tender skin of her arm.

"Ahh!" she cried, clutching at her shoulder as the hot liquid stung her.

Papa spun around instantly, his spatula clattering to the floor. "That's enough!" he thundered, his voice shaking the walls. He crossed the kitchen in three strides, positioning himself between Maddie and her father. "You've done enough damage this morning. Sit down. Now."

Her father's chest heaved, his face twisted with anger and shame, but Papa's stance left no room for argument. He backed down with a muttered curse and dropped heavily into his chair.

Papa turned back to Maddie, his expression softening. "Come here, sweetheart," he said gently. He scooped her up into his arms, careful not to touch the burned skin, and carried her to the sink. "We're going to fix you right up."

Maddie's mom was already on her feet, her face pale as she abandoned her coffee cup and hurried to her daughter's side. "Oh, baby," she whispered, her voice trembling. "Let me see."

Together, they worked as a quiet team, Papa running cool water gently over Maddie's shoulder while Mom fetched a soft towel and dabbed at the edges of the burn. Maddie whimpered, her little fingers clutching me tightly against her chest.

"It's okay," Papa murmured softly. "Papa's got you. We'll make it better."

Mom knelt beside them, brushing Maddie's damp hair back from her forehead. "You're going to be okay, sweetheart. I'm so sorry this happened."

"It hurts," Maddie sniffled, pressing her face against my bonnet.

"I know, baby," Mom whispered, kissing her cheek. "I know."

When the worst of the sting had faded, Papa carefully wrapped her shoulder in a cool, damp cloth. "There," he said quietly. "That should help. We'll keep an eye on it today."

Maddie sniffled once more and nodded, her face still pressed into me. The kitchen was silent except for the soft hiss of the stove and the faint crackle of bacon still cooking. The smell of pancakes lingered, but it was changed now, tinged with bitterness and pain.

Papa exhaled slowly, his jaw tight as he glanced over his shoulder at the man slumped at the table. "No more outbursts," he said, his tone calm but sharp as steel. "Not in front of them, I hope you're proud of yourself." He looked from him to Maddie.

No one answered. But Papa didn't need a reply. He turned back to Maddie and kissed the top of her head. "You're safe, my girl. You're safe."

And as Maddie buried her tear-streaked face against me, I understood in my seams and stitches just how much she needed that love, how desperately she clung to it when the world around her felt like it could break apart at any second.

Chapter Seven

The world outside had been transformed overnight. A thick blanket of snow lay across the mountainside, glittering in the pale winter sun like a field of diamonds. The bare branches of the maples and birches stretched toward the sky, their tips dusted white, and the dirt road that wound past their little house had turned into a soft ribbon of snow, perfect for boots and sleds alike.

Papa thought fresh air would do everyone good before he headed home. "We need one last adventure," he'd said that morning, pulling on his heavy coat and wool hat. "And I know just the place."

So after breakfast, he and Mom bundled Maddie and Wyatt into layers of scarves, hats, and mittens. Maddie tugged on her favorite pair, the silly puppet mittens her Great Aunt made her every Christmas. Each one had big googly eyes and a yarn mouth stitched into a smile. The mouths were cleverly designed so that when Maddie wiggled her fingers inside, the mittens' "mouths" opened and closed like talking puppets. Every year a new pair arrived to replace the ones she had worn out from so much play, and she loved them most of all because they made her laugh, even on the coldest days.

She tucked me safely under her arm, wrapped snug in one of her doll blankets so I wouldn't "get cold." "You're coming too, Jane," she whispered. "I want you to see everything."

The four of them followed the narrow snow-covered road that wound downhill from the house. The cold bit at their cheeks, but the air was crisp and clean, and the sunlight spilled over the Green Mountains in the distance, painting them in shades of deep green and silver.

"Look, Papa!" Maddie cried, pointing to a flash of bright blue as a jay darted from tree to tree.

"Blue jay," Papa said with a smile. "Always noisy, always nosy."

"And there's a cardinal!" Mom called from behind them, pointing to a red streak in the branches. "My favorite."

The snow crunched beneath their boots as they walked, and Maddie held me close the whole way, lifting me every so often to "show" me the view. "See that, Jane? That's the Green Mountains," she whispered into the cold air. "They're even prettier in the snow."

They soon reached the edge of the wide, open cornfield. The tall stalks were gone, leaving behind sweeping white hills that sloped gently toward the valley below. It was their favorite winter spot, a place where the wind was sharp and the laughter echoed against the hills.

"Perfect sledding day," Papa declared, setting down the old wooden sled he had pulled from the shed that morning. Its paint was faded, but its runners still gleamed, polished smooth from decades of use.

"Me first!" Wyatt shouted, hopping on eagerly.

Papa chuckled. "Hold on tight, speed racer." He gave the sled a mighty push, and Wyatt whooped as he flew down the hill, snow spraying in his wake.

Maddie giggled and bounced on her boots, holding me up to watch. "Did you see that, Jane? He's going so fast!"

Her turn was next. Papa helped her settle onto the sled, tucking me securely into her lap. "Ready?" he asked, his warm breath puffing white in the air.

"Ready!" she squealed.

With a strong push, Papa sent them gliding down the hill. The wind rushed against Maddie's face as the sled flew over the snow, faster and faster, until the world blurred into white and blue. She laughed, the sound ringing out across the field, and held me high above her head.

"Look, Jane! We're flying!" she shouted joyfully. Then, with a burst of giggles, she added, "Just like Tinker Bell and Peter Pan!"

At the bottom of the hill, she tumbled gently into the snow with a soft whoosh, landing on her back with me still clutched tight in her mittened hands. She lifted one mitten and wiggled her fingers, making the yarn "mouth" open and close. "Did you like that?" she asked the mitten puppet in a high, silly voice. Then she turned to the other hand and wiggled it too. "I did! Let's go again!"

She burst into giggles, and I could feel the joy radiating from her. For that moment, there was just laughter, snow, and silly talking mittens.

They spent the afternoon racing and laughing, taking turns on the sled, building small snowmen along the edge of the field, and stopping often to catch their breath and admire the view. The Green Mountains rose tall and proud behind them, their forested slopes dusted white, a perfect backdrop to their little adventure.

Papa pulled out his camera, its leather strap slung over his shoulder, and snapped picture after picture. Maddie and Wyatt posed with their sled at the top of the hill, Mom knelt in the snow between them, and Papa set the timer so he could join the group shot too. Maddie held me proudly in the photos, insisting I be in every single one.

"This one," Papa said after snapping the last picture, "this one's going on the mantle."

The afternoon sun began to dip low, painting the snow in shades of gold and pink. As they trudged back up the hill one last time, Maddie grew quiet, holding me close against her chest. "I don't want today to end," she whispered to me. "Papa's leaving soon."

Papa must have heard her, because he reached down and lifted her up into his arms. "I know, Maddie-girl," he said softly, kissing her cold cheek. "But you and Wyatt gave me the best send-off I could ask for. And you know what? I'll be back before you know it."

Maddie nodded against his shoulder, but she didn't let go of me. I could feel her heartbeat through the layers of wool and cotton, steady, warm, and clinging tightly to this perfect, fleeting moment.

When they returned home, cheeks rosy and boots soaked through from the snow, Mom set a pot on the old gas stove and filled the kitchen with the sweet scent of cocoa. "Hot chocolate for everyone," she announced. Maddie and Wyatt climbed up onto the kitchen chairs, their hands wrapped around warm mugs, and Papa dropped a handful of tiny marshmallows into each one. They bobbed and melted into little sugary clouds on top.

"Perfect after-sledding treat," Papa said with a wink, raising his mug.

Maddie giggled and took a big sip, the warmth spreading through her chest and chasing away the winter chill. "Mmm… this is the best," she whispered, looking down at me in her lap. "Did you like sledding too, Jane?"

It was their last adventure before Papa had to go home, an afternoon of laughter, snow, and sweet cocoa. I was there, nestled against Maddie's heart, seeing her world blanketed in snow and filled, just for a little while, with nothing but love.

Chapter Eight

That night, the house felt softer. The chill of the winter air had been chased away by the warmth of hot chocolate and the glow from the old wood stove, and the laughter from sledding still lingered in every corner. Even the usual heaviness that sometimes clung to the walls seemed to have lifted, just for now.

After dinner, Papa called Maddie and Wyatt into the living room. "Alright, you two," he said with a playful grin, "I think there's time for one more story before bed."

Maddie's eyes lit up instantly. "Please, Papa, read from the orange book!" she begged, hopping on her toes.

Papa chuckled. "You already know which one I was thinking of."

He walked over to the small wooden shelf near the old armchair and pulled down a worn, orange hardcover book. Its corners were frayed, and the spine was cracked from years of turning pages, but to Maddie, it was a treasure. It had once belonged to her mom when she was a little girl. An encyclopedia anthology of nursery rhymes and fairy tales, filled with stories that had been told and retold for generations.

Maddie gasped when she saw it. "The orange book!" she squealed, clapping her hands together. "Can we read Snow White and Rose Red?"

"You know it," Papa said, settling into the armchair and flipping carefully through the well-worn pages.

Before he began, Maddie suddenly darted up the stairs. "Wait! I need to get everyone!" she called over her shoulder.

A few moments later, she came back down, her arms full. Rabberta dangled from one hand, Trisha cradled gently in the other. "They want to hear the story too," she announced seriously as she marched back into the living room.

She placed Rabberta carefully on the pillow next to her on the floor, set Trisha in her little doll crib nearby, and held me close under her arm. "Okay, everyone," she said with importance. "Papa's reading now. Pay attention."

I did. Every word.

Papa's deep voice carried the story through the room like a lullaby. He read of the two kind sisters, Snow White and Rose Red, who helped a bear in the winter and showed kindness even when the world around them was cold. As he spoke, I watched Maddie's eyes widen with wonder. They sparkled with every twist of the tale, her small body leaning closer with each turn of the page.

When the bear revealed his true identity, she gasped softly, even though she had heard the story a dozen times before. "I love this part," she whispered to me, hugging me close.

Papa smiled over the top of the book. "I know you do, Maddie-girl."

By the time the story ended and the bear-prince and the sisters lived happily ever after, Maddie was resting her head on my soft bonnet, her eyelids growing heavy. Papa closed the orange book gently and set it back on the shelf, its cover glowing faintly in the firelight.

"Alright, you two," Papa said softly, his voice warm. "Time for bed."

He scooped Wyatt up first, carrying him up the stairs and into his room, pulling the blanket up under his chin. "Goodnight, big guy," he said softly, kissing his forehead.

"'Night, Papa," Wyatt mumbled, already half-asleep.

Then Papa led Maddie by the hand into her little room at the end of the hallway. She placed Rabberta and Trisha back in their spots and climbed into bed with me still tucked under her arm. Papa pulled the quilt up around her small body and smoothed her hair away from her face.

"Goodnight, my Maddie-girl," he whispered. "Sweet dreams. Dream about sledding and stories and all the good things waiting for you tomorrow."

"Goodnight, Papa," Maddie murmured sleepily, her voice warm and content. "I love you."

"I love you too," he said, pressing a gentle kiss to her forehead before turning off the light.

The house settled into stillness, the soft crackle of the wood stove downstairs the only sound. Maddie shifted once, hugging me close under her chin, then went still. A small smile curved across her lips as she drifted into dreams. Dreams of snowy hills, warm cocoa, and days spent with the people she loved most.

I stayed awake a little longer, listening to her soft breaths and watching the peaceful rise and fall of her chest. Her world wasn't always easy, but tonight, just for tonight, it was gentle. Safe. And as the stars glittered outside the window and the old orange book rested quietly on the shelf, I knew this was a memory Maddie would carry with her forever.

Chapter Nine

Morning came quietly, with pale winter sunlight spilling across the frosted windows and the smell of wood smoke drifting from the stove. The house was still for a moment. That gentle, sleepy kind of stillness that only comes on cold mornings, until the sound of clinking pans drifted from the kitchen.

"Up and at 'em," Papa called from downstairs, his voice warm and steady. "Breakfast is almost ready!"

Maddie rubbed her eyes and clutched me close as she sat up. The memories of sledding and stories from the day before lingered in her chest like a soft glow, but underneath them was something heavier, the knowing that Papa was leaving today.

She got dressed slowly, taking extra care that morning. From the small dresser in the corner of her chilly white room, she chose her favorite shirt, the one with Ariel from The Little Mermaid on the front. Ariel was her favorite princess, and Maddie liked to think they had a lot in common. They were both dreamers, both searching for a world that felt bigger and brighter than the one they knew. Pulling the shirt over her head made her feel a little braver, a little closer to that kind of magic.

She carefully brushed her hair, tugging the brush through the tangles with determination. "I don't want him to go, Jane," she whispered to me as she buttoned her pants. "I wish he could stay forever."

Downstairs, the kitchen was filled with the comforting scent of frying eggs and toasted bread. Papa was at the old gas stove, humming softly as he cooked. Mom stood beside him with a spatula, helping plate the food. This was their special breakfast, egg toast, a fried egg cooked in the center of a hole cut into a slice of bread. It was Maddie's favorite, a "Mom breakfast special" she looked forward to whenever mornings felt important.

"Morning, sleepyheads," Papa said as Maddie and Wyatt shuffled into the kitchen. "Just in time. Breakfast is served."

"Thanks, Papa," Maddie said softly, sliding into her chair.

Her dad was already there, sitting at the table in silence. He didn't say a word to Papa or us. He didn't even look at any of us. A cigarette smoldered between his fingers, Marlboro smoke curling lazily in the air, and his mug of coffee sat in front of him, half-finished and black. He took a slow sip, flicked the ash into an old tray, and stared out the window like no one else was in the room.

Papa didn't comment. He never did. He simply carried on, setting plates on the table and smiling down at Maddie and Wyatt as if the heavy silence didn't exist. "Eat up, kids," he said cheerfully. "We've got a big day of… well, me heading home." His voice wavered just slightly at the end, and Maddie caught it.

Breakfast passed with small conversation. Papa asking Wyatt about school, Maddie telling him about the story they'd read, Mom quietly sipping her coffee with tired eyes. The clink of forks and the low hum of the stove filled the space where her dad's silence sat like a cold shadow.

When the plates were empty and the mugs were rinsed, Papa stood and zipped up his heavy winter coat. "Well," he said, turning to the kids with a smile that didn't quite reach his eyes, "I guess it's time for me to hit the road."

Maddie's stomach sank. She clutched me tighter.

"Do you really have to go?" she whispered, her voice trembling.

Papa knelt down in front of her so they were eye to eye. "I do, Maddie-girl," he said gently. "But you listen to me, I'm just a phone call away. And I'll be back before you know it, ready for another sledding race down that big hill."

Tears welled in Maddie's eyes, and she threw her arms around his neck. "I'm gonna miss you, Papa."

"I'm gonna miss you too, sweetheart," he whispered into her hair, hugging her tight. "But I'm always here." He tapped her chest softly over her heart. "Right here. Always."

Wyatt shuffled over, trying to act tough but hugging Papa just as hard. "Bye, Papa," he said, his voice small.

"Bye, champ. Take care of your sister, okay?"

"I will."

Mom walked over, wrapping Papa in a quiet embrace. "Drive safe," she murmured. There was something in her voice, gratitude, maybe, or longing, but she didn't say anything more.

Papa nodded and turned toward the door. Maddie followed him, still holding me close, her mittened hands twisting in the hem of his coat as if letting go would make him disappear. He crouched down one last time at the door, brushing a tear from her cheek with his thumb.

"You be brave, Maddie-girl," he said softly. "And take care of Jane for me."

"I will," she whispered, her voice catching.

Then he kissed her forehead, gave Wyatt's shoulder a squeeze, and stepped out into the cold.

The screen door creaked shut behind him, and the rumble of his truck engine soon faded down the snow-lined road. Maddie stood in the doorway long after he was gone, clutching me tight against her chest, watching the trail his tires left behind in the snow.

The kitchen behind her felt heavier again, the clink of her dad's coffee cup, the faint smell of cigarette smoke, but she held on to the warmth Papa left behind. It lingered like sunlight in her chest, soft and steady, even as the winter morning stretched on without him.

Chapter Ten

The house was unusually calm that day. After Papa's truck disappeared down the snowy road and the morning melted into afternoon, no one raised their voice. No dishes slammed. No doors were slammed in anger. It was the kind of quiet that felt almost fragile, like a snowflake resting gently on a mitten. Soft, rare, and easily broken.

Maddie wandered from room to room with me tucked under her arm, unsure what to do with herself. She missed Papa already. But when she heard the faint buzz of tools and the rhythmic tap-tap-tap of a hammer coming from the basement, curiosity tugged her toward the narrow wooden stairs.

"Come on, Jane," she whispered, hugging me close. "Let's go see what Daddy's doing."

The air grew cooler as she descended the creaky steps, and a musty scent met her nose. The damp, earthy smell of old wood, cool stone, and years of sawdust. It was an odd smell, but one Maddie liked. It reminded her of hidden places and quiet corners, and for some reason, it always made her smile.

The basement wasn't big, but to Maddie, it felt like a whole different world, one full of tools and scraps of wood, half-finished projects and jars of nails that glimmered like treasure.

Her dad was hunched over his workbench, wood shavings scattered around his boots. He looked up when he heard her small footsteps.

"Well, hey there, peanut," he said, his voice softer than usual. "What are you doing down here?"

"I wanted to see what you're working on," Maddie said, hugging me tighter and peering over the edge of the bench.

He wiped his hands on a rag and held up a smooth, carved piece of wood. "Making a plant hanger for your mom. Something she's been asking me for."

Maddie's blue eyes widened. "It's pretty," she said. "Can I watch?"

"Of course." He pulled an old wooden stool over and patted the seat beside him. "Hop on up, Maddie-girl."

Maddie climbed onto the stool, setting me gently on her lap so I could "see" too. All around her were tools of every shape and size, hammers, screwdrivers, sandpaper, a chisel, a small hand saw, even a little wooden mallet.

"What's that one?" she asked, pointing.

"That," he said, picking up a thin, sharp tool, "is a chisel. It helps me carve the wood and shape it just right."

"And that one?" she asked, pointing again.

"This one's a clamp," he explained, demonstrating how it held the wood still while he worked. "It's like a helper with strong hands."

Maddie giggled. "I like that one."

Before long, she was mimicking his movements with scraps of wood he set aside for her, pretending she was fixing teeth instead of sanding boards. "Hold still, sir," she said in a mock-serious voice, poking a dowel with the tip of a screwdriver. "Your cavity needs filling."

Her dad laughed, a sound that startled her at first because it was so rare. "A dentist, huh? Maybe that's what you'll be when you grow up."

"Maybe," she said, grinning. "But I like building things too. Like you."

He smiled at that, a small, genuine smile that didn't look tired or angry. "Then I'll have to teach you everything I know."

And he did. For the next hour, he showed her how to sand the wood in smooth, even strokes, how to measure with a tape and mark the wood just right, and how to line up the nails before hammering them in. He even guided her small hands as she gently tapped a nail into place.

"There you go," he said proudly. "You've got a natural talent."

Maddie beamed, her cheeks pink with pride. "Thanks, Daddy."

Side by side, they worked, he on his plant hanger, she on her imaginary teeth, and the basement filled with the soft scrape of sandpaper and the rhythmic tap-tap of the hammer. It was the kind of afternoon Maddie wished they could have more often. Calm. Full of small smiles and shared moments.

After a lovely afternoon together, they finally climbed back up the creaky basement stairs. Her dad wiped his hands on a rag and headed into the kitchen, cracking open a can of Budweiser with a familiar psssht. Maddie carried me into the living room and popped her favorite movie, The Little Mermaid, into the old VCR.

I could see why she loved it so much, the colorful fish darting across the screen, the cheerful songs that filled the room, and the happy ending where everything turned out all right. Maddie sang softly along with Ariel, her eyes shining with wonder, and for a little while, the world around us felt just as magical as the one on the screen.

Chapter Eleven

The late afternoon sun streamed softly through Maddie's small bedroom window, painting golden squares across the worn wooden floor. The heat from the wood stove downstairs barely reached this far, but Maddie didn't seem to mind. She had piled blankets and pillows into a cozy nest near her bed, and the coolness in the air only made it feel more magical, like the deep waters of the ocean she was about to explore.

With The Little Mermaid still swirling in her head, Maddie decided her room was no longer a small, drafty space on the second floor of a creaky old house. No, today it was the bottom of the sea. And she was a mermaid princess.

She placed Rabberta near the foot of her bed. "You're Flounder," she told the pink bunny with a solemn nod. "You're my best underwater friend." Then she tucked Trisha into her doll crib and announced, "And you're Sebastian. You make sure we don't get in trouble."

Finally, she set me gently on her pillow, smoothing my pink lace dress. "And you, Jane," she said, her blue eyes sparkling, "you're Scuttle the seagull. You know everything."

The game had begun.

Maddie hummed softly at first, twirling across the room as if her feet were fins gliding through the sea. Then, unable to hold it in any longer, she threw her head back and belted out Ariel's most famous song from the top of her lungs, her little voice filling the small room with passion and joy.

She spun in wide, clumsy circles, her arms stretched high above her head as if reaching for the surface of the ocean itself. Her laughter mixed with the song as she pretended to swim through coral reefs and collect treasures from shipwrecks.

"Look, everyone!" she called out mid-spin, holding her arms out dramatically. "I'm a mermaid princess! And one day, I'm going to explore the world above!"

She plopped down on her blanket "reef" and sighed dreamily, staring up at the ceiling as if it were the surface of the sea. "I bet there are so many things up there. Books and castles and real people to talk to." Then she giggled and added, "And maybe even forks you can comb your hair with!"

Rabberta and Trisha "replied" in their usual way, with Maddie doing all the voices.

"Be careful, Maddie-mermaid!" Trisha squeaked. "The human world is dangerous!"

"Oh, hush!" she scolded in Rabberta's voice. "Let her dream a little!"

Maddie laughed and clutched me close, whispering, "What do you think, Jane? Should I go see what's up there?" She waited a beat as if listening for my answer, then nodded. "I think so too."

But then her tone softened, and her little mermaid voice grew wistful. "If I go to the human world," she told Rabberta and Trisha softly, "I'll miss everyone down here so much. I'll miss my friends… and Papa… and Mom." She hugged me tighter, her voice barely a whisper now. "But maybe they'll still love me, even if I'm far away."

Her pretend play shifted into storytelling as she swam from one corner of the room to the other, describing all the adventures she and her toy friends would have. They found treasure chests (an old shoe box under her bed), danced with dolphins (a pillow she pushed across the floor), and even built a magical palace out of blocks near her dresser.

And through it all, she talked. About Papa and how much fun the sledding had been, about helping her dad in the basement, and about how she wished days like that could last forever. "It was a good day, wasn't it?" she asked Rabberta, who nodded sagely in Maddie's imagination. "I hope tomorrow is like this too."

From my spot on the pillow, I watched her with quiet wonder. This was Maddie in her truest form, a bright, curious, wildly imaginative little girl whose heart was bigger than the world she lived in. And even when that world wasn't always kind, she still found ways to fill it with magic.

As the last light of day faded into twilight, Maddie collapsed onto her bed in a happy, tangled heap of blankets, toys, and giggles. "Whew," she sighed dramatically, "being a mermaid princess is hard work."

A little while later, soft footsteps padded up the stairs, and Maddie's bedroom door creaked open. Her mom stepped inside, still smelling faintly of soap from her shower, and smiled. "Hey, my little mermaid," she said gently. "Ready for a bedtime story?"

Maddie's eyes lit up. Mom didn't get to tuck her in very often, she was usually still at work by the time bedtime came around. But when she was home, it felt special.

"Can we read the orange book again?" Maddie asked hopefully.

"Of course we can," Mom said, settling beside her on the bed and pulling the worn orange book from the shelf. She read softly by the dim glow of the bedside lamp, her voice soothing and warm as the familiar stories filled the room once again.

When the story ended, Mom tucked the blankets snugly around Maddie and wrapped her in a hug that was warm and steady, the kind of hug that made everything feel okay, no matter what. Maddie closed her eyes, sinking into the embrace. Her mom's arms were her safest place.

"I love you, Mommy," she whispered sleepily.

"I love you too, sweetheart," Mom whispered back, brushing a strand of hair from Maddie's forehead and kissing her goodnight.

The room grew quiet as the lamp clicked off. Maddie clutched me close under her chin, her heart still humming with mermaid songs and storybook magic. And as her breathing slowed and the stars blinked softly outside her window, she drifted into dreams. Dreams of oceans, adventures, and the people she loved most.

Chapter Twelve

The night after Papa left was always the hardest.

The house felt different, heavier, darker. As if all the warmth he'd brought with him had left with his truck. Maddie fell asleep hugging me tight, her heart aching with how much she already missed him. But sleep didn't last long.

A scream shattered the silence.

Maddie's eyes flew open, her whole body tensing as the sound echoed up the stairs. I could feel the change in her heartbeat, fast and shaky. She clutched me tighter, pressing me to her chest as if I could block out the noise.

Another scream. Louder this time. It was her mother.

Maddie slipped out of bed and crept to the door, her bare feet silent on the cold floor. As she cracked it open, she saw Wyatt just ahead of her, creeping down the stairs to look into the darkness below.

"Wyatt," she whispered, her voice trembling. "Come back."

But before he could, another scream tore through the house, followed by the crash of something breaking. Maddie's heart hammered in her chest.

Wyatt didn't listen. He bolted down the stairs toward the sound. Maddie followed slowly, clutching me so tightly I thought my seams might burst.

"Leave him alone!" her mother shouted. There was a heavy thump that shook the floor. Maddie froze, her breath catching in her throat.

Then she heard her mother again, her voice desperate and terrified. "Stop it! Please, stop!"

Maddie crept down two more steps where she saw Wyatt disappear around the corner into the living room, into the space where their mom and dad were. The chaos is growing louder.

"Wyatt, come back!" she whispered, but her voice was too small, too scared to carry over the shouting.

Peeking around the corner, Maddie's breath caught in a silent gasp.

Wyatt was on the floor. Her father stood over him, rage twisting his face, one hand raised high in the air. Maddie's stomach turned cold. She couldn't move. Couldn't speak.

"Stop!" Mom screamed again as she threw herself between them, pushing Wyatt back toward the stairs. "Go upstairs! Go now!"

Her mother's eyes found Maddie's then, wild, terrified eyes that made her heart feel like it would break. "Take Jane and go, Maddie!" she shouted. "Lock the door and don't come out!"

Wyatt scrambled to his feet and grabbed Maddie's hand. "Come on!" he hissed, pulling her toward the stairs. She stumbled as they climbed, my soft body clutched in her small hands, her heart pounding so hard she could hear it in her ears.

They ran into Maddie's room and slammed the door shut. Wyatt turned the lock and then pulled her under the bed with him, the two of them curling into a tight ball in the darkness.

Downstairs, the sounds grew louder. More screaming. More crashing. And then the worst of all, the unmistakable sounds of something unthinkable happening.

Maddie pressed me against her chest, sobbing silently as tears streamed down her cheeks. "I'm scared, Jane," she whispered, her voice shaking. "I'm so scared."

I could feel the tremors in her small body as she shook and cried, Wyatt's arm wrapped protectively around her. They stayed there, hidden in the dark space beneath the bed, listening helplessly to the chaos below.

Every scream from their mother felt like a knife in Maddie's chest. Every crash made her flinch harder. And every second that passed made the house feel less like a home and more like a place she needed to escape from.

All she could do was hold me tight, her one small comfort in a night that had none, and pray for the noise to stop.

Chapter Thirteen

The house was finally quiet.

The screams had faded, the crashing had stopped, and only silence filled the dark rooms now. It wasn't a peaceful silence, not the soft, sleepy kind that used to settle over the house on nights when Papa told stories by the wood stove. This silence was heavy and fragile, the kind that hummed in your chest and left your ears ringing.

Eventually, Maddie and Wyatt crawled out from under the bed. Their faces were streaked with tears, their bodies exhausted from fear and crying. They climbed into Maddie's small twin bed and curled up together under the blankets, Wyatt's arm protectively around his little sister. Maddie still held me tight against her chest, her small hands trembling even as her breathing slowed.

And finally, mercifully, sleep came.

That's when the Night Council gathered.

One by one, the toys stirred in the moonlight that spilled softly through the frosted windowpane. Rabberta hopped closer on her soft pink paws, her floppy ears swaying with each gentle bounce. Her fur, once bright and new, was now faded in places from years of hugs and tears, but her stitched-on smile never changed.

Trisha sat up in her doll crib, straightening the little blanket around her cloth body. She was Maddie's first baby doll, her oldest friend. She carried the quiet wisdom of all the bedtime stories, whispered secrets, and long nights she'd witnessed.

And I sat perched on Maddie's chest, still and listening.

"It was another bad one tonight," Rabberta said softly, her button eyes glistening in the moonlight. "Worse than the last."

"They always are when Papa leaves," Trisha replied, her voice gentle but tired. "He tries harder when Papa's here. Pretends to be better. But the moment Papa's gone…" She glanced toward the closed bedroom door, where shadows stretched across the floor. "The monster comes back."

I looked between them, my fabric heart aching. "Does this happen often?" I asked quietly.

Rabberta nodded sadly. "Too often. It's been like this for as long as I can remember. Maddie was barely more than a baby the first time I heard her crying in the dark after one of their fights."

"And Wyatt…" Trisha added softly, "he stopped playing like a child long before he should have. He tries to protect her. He shouldn't have to, but he does."

"Children shouldn't live like this," I whispered.

"No," Rabberta agreed, her voice trembling. "But they do. They've learned how to hide, how to be silent, how to stay small and safe when the storm comes."

"They grew up faster than they should have," Trisha said. "And not because they wanted to. Because they had to."

The room fell silent again, the weight of their words sinking deep into the quiet.

I looked down at Maddie's sleeping face. Her cheeks were still damp with tears, her brow creased even in sleep. Wyatt stirred beside her, murmuring something I couldn't understand, his small hand never letting go of hers.

"She has so much light inside her," I said softly. "So much imagination. So much love. It shouldn't have to be buried under fear."

Rabberta hopped closer and nuzzled against my side. "That's why we're here, Jane. To be her safe place when the world isn't. To listen when she talks. To remind her that love still exists, even in the darkness."

I nodded. I understood now. My purpose here was bigger than tea parties and make-believe. I was here to help hold her together, to be a constant in a world that shifted like sand beneath her feet.

Gently, I reached up with my small stitched hand and wiped away the lingering tears from Maddie's cheeks. Her face softened in her sleep, and for the first time since the screaming stopped, her breathing grew calm and steady.

The Night Council sat together in silence for a long time, watching over Maddie and Wyatt as they slept curled up like two small survivors after a storm. The house might have been quiet now, but we all knew this wasn't the end.

Before the night faded, we each took our places. Rabberta near the door, Trisha by the window, and me still resting against Maddie's heart. We stood guard as best we could, keeping watch over her and Wyatt, keeping the shadows at bay.

And as the moon crossed the sky and the hours crept by, we guarded Maddie's door and kept the rest of the night safe.

Chapter Fourteen

A few days later, the holidays were over, and school was starting again. The decorations were still up in the house, but they looked a little duller now, like they were tired too.

Maddie and Wyatt stood side by side at the bottom of their long, snowy driveway, their breath puffing white clouds into the cold Vermont air. Both wore secondhand snow gear they had gotten for Christmas, coats with slightly frayed cuffs, mismatched mittens, and boots that had belonged to someone else before them. Maddie's coat was pink, but the color had faded in places, and one of the buttons was shaped like a heart while the others were plain circles.

Maddie didn't mind. She liked the heart button.

She hugged me close under her arm as the school bus rumbled up the road, the sound of chains clinking against the icy tires. Wyatt nudged her with his elbow. "Here it comes," he said.

The bus hissed to a stop, and the doors creaked open. Wyatt hopped up the steps first, giving the driver a quick nod before heading straight to the back, where his friends were calling him over. Maddie followed quietly, climbing the big steps with a bit of effort and finding a seat in the middle of the bus. She slid into it and set me gently on her lap, looking out the frosted window as the bus pulled away.

As the snow-covered trees and farm fields passed by, she started to hum softly. Then, almost without realizing it, she began to sing one of her favorite songs from the movie "Annie" that always gave her hope for better tomorrows.

Her voice was small but hopeful, carrying the tune like a secret she shared only with me.

A few stops later, the bus door opened again, and a girl with long black hair and brand-new winter clothes climbed aboard. Her jacket was shiny and bright, and her boots looked like they had never touched snow before. She glanced around, then made her way toward Maddie's seat.

"Hi," the girl said, sliding in beside her. "I'm Anna."

"Hi," Maddie said shyly, her voice barely above a whisper.

For a moment, the conversation was pleasant. Anna asked about Maddie's Christmas and if she was excited to be back at school. Maddie nodded and told her about the sledding trip with Papa and how much she liked her new doll, me.

Anna smiled and looked Maddie up and down. "That's a nice coat," she said.

Maddie's face lit up. "Thank you," she said brightly, smoothing the faded fabric with her mittened hands. "It was a Christmas present."

But Anna's smile shifted, it wasn't kind anymore. It was sharp, mean. "Yeah," she said with a small laugh. "It used to be mine. My mom donated it to the church last year."

Maddie blinked, unsure how to respond.

"Oh wow, you're wearing my old coat!" Anna said louder now, turning so the girls in the row behind them could hear. "Guess your family can't afford new clothes."

The other girls giggled. One of them whispered something, and they all laughed harder.

Maddie's chest tightened. The warmth drained from her face, replaced by a deep, stinging shame. She looked down at her lap, blinking back tears. "I like my coat," she said softly, but her voice cracked as the tears came anyway.

Wyatt, from the back of the bus, noticed her shoulders shaking. He stood up, weaving through the rows until he reached her seat. "Maddie," he said gently, crouching beside her. "Are you okay?"

Maddie nodded quickly, even though tears streaked her cheeks. "I'm fine," she whispered, clutching me tight.

The girls behind them snickered again. Wyatt turned to Anna. "What did you say to her?" he demanded.

Anna crossed her arms. "I just said she's wearing my old coat. It's true."

Wyatt's jaw clenched. "You think you're better than her because you got new clothes?"

Anna shrugged, smirking. "Well… yeah."

Before anyone could stop him, Wyatt's fist flew forward and connected squarely with Anna's nose. A gasp rippled through the bus as Anna shrieked, her hands flying to her face as blood trickled between her fingers.

The bus lurched as the driver slammed the brakes, shouting over the chaos, "Enough! That's enough!"

She marched down the aisle, her face red with anger. "Wyatt Ryder!" she barked. "Front seat. Now."

"But she was making fun of Maddie!" Wyatt tried to explain, pointing at Anna, who was sobbing into a tissue now. "She called her poor and—"

"I don't want to hear it," the driver snapped, cutting him off. "Violence is never the answer. Your parents will be called."

Wyatt's face flushed hot with anger and frustration, but he did as he was told. He stomped to the very front of the bus and dropped into the first seat, his fists still clenched. Maddie watched him go, her heart twisting. He had only been trying to protect her.

The rest of the ride was tense and silent. Maddie kept her eyes fixed on the snowy landscape outside, tears still slipping down her cheeks as the girls behind her whispered and giggled. She pressed me close to her chest and tried to disappear into the seat.

When the bus finally arrived at school, Wyatt was marched straight to the principal's office, and Maddie slipped quietly into her classroom. It was show-and-tell day, the first one of the new year, and even though her stomach was in knots, she held me close and waited for her turn.

When the teacher called her name, Maddie stood at the front of the room, cheeks still pink from crying. She held me up for the class to see.

"This is Jane," she said softly. "She's my doll. My papa gave her to me for Christmas, and she's my best friend."

The room was quiet for a moment, and then a few kids smiled. Someone even said, "She's pretty."

And for the first time that day, Maddie felt a little warmth return to her chest. She hugged me close as she walked back to her seat, whispering so only I could hear:

"At least I still have you."

Chapter Fifteen

The rest of the school day went well. Maddie had always loved school. She especially loved music, writing, and reading. They were like little doorways into brighter worlds. Math, on the other hand, wasn't her favorite, but she did her best with it anyway.

When the final bell rang, she lined up with the other students to wait for the buses. The afternoon ride home was much quieter than the morning had been, and this time there was a different driver. Mr. Nelson, a kind older man with gentle eyes and a warm smile, was behind the wheel. He always reminded Maddie a little of Papa. He was patient, and kind.

Her and Wyatt's stop was the last one of the day, and as always, Mr. Nelson drove them all the way up the long driveway so they wouldn't have to walk through the cold. "Have a good night, you two," he said as they climbed down the steps. Maddie smiled and waved.

Inside, the house was still and dim. Their father was sprawled on the couch, snoring softly, a half-empty can of Budweiser teetering on the edge of the coffee table. Beside it lay a rubber band and a used needle. Maddie stared at it for a moment, her small chest tightening. They wouldn't be seeing much of him tonight, not like this.

Mom was at work and wouldn't be home until after they were asleep. So, as usual, Wyatt took charge. He spread his books across the kitchen table and started on his homework while Maddie colored quietly beside him. When he finished, he rummaged through the cupboards and found a box of macaroni and cheese. "Dinner," he announced with a crooked smile.

They spoke in whispers as they worked, trying to keep the kitchen as quiet as possible. Waking Dad never ended well.

But then it happened, a slip, a small mistake. Maddie was carrying her empty plate to the sink when it slipped from her hands and shattered on the floor.

The sound broke the silence like a gunshot.

From the living room came a deep, slurred growl. "What the hell was that?"

Maddie froze. Wyatt's face went pale.

Their father stumbled into the kitchen, his eyes glassy and unfocused, anger radiating from him like heat. He stared down at the broken plate, then at Maddie. "Did you do this?" he barked.

"It was an accident," Maddie whispered.

"An accident?" he snapped. "We work hard for what we have, and you break it like it's nothing?"

Wyatt muttered under his breath, too low to mean to be heard. "You don't even work…"

But he was heard.

Their father's head whipped around. "What did you say?"

Wyatt swallowed hard. "Nothing."

He was grabbed by the collar and yanked forward. "Say it again!"

"I didn't—"

The crack of a slap cut through the air. Wyatt stumbled back, clutching his cheek, his eyes wide with shock and fury.

Then their father turned to Maddie. The room seemed to shrink, the air disappearing from her lungs.

"Turn around," he said coldly.

Maddie's heart pounded. She clutched me so tightly it hurt, but she did as she was told, her small body trembling.

What followed wasn't something I could describe in words, but it included the sharp snap of a belt and the heavy weight of punishment that no child should ever know. Maddie stood still through all of it, biting her lip so hard it nearly bled, determined not to cry. Because crying always made it worse.

When it was over, the house was silent again. Maddie and Wyatt retreated upstairs without a word. They didn't speak until they were safe inside Maddie's room, the door locked behind them.

Wyatt guided her gently to the bed. "Let me see," he whispered. Maddie hesitated, her hands shaking, but slowly turned around and lifted the back of her shirt. Wyatt's breath caught. "It's okay," he said softly, though his voice was trembling. "I've got you."

He went to the small closet and rummaged through the top shelf until he found an old shoebox with a few bandages, a washcloth, and a nearly empty bottle of antiseptic. It wasn't much, but it was all they had.

Wyatt dampened the cloth and began carefully cleaning the welts on Maddie's skin. She winced but didn't make a sound. His hands were gentle, far gentler than any adult's had been lately.

"I'm sorry," Wyatt whispered as he worked. "I shouldn't have said anything. I made it worse."

Maddie shook her head. "It's not your fault," she said quietly. "It's never your fault."

He finished tending to her wounds and helped her into her softest pajamas, the ones with the faded pink bunnies on them. Then he tucked the blankets around her and placed me gently in her arms.

"I'll stay here tonight," he said, sliding onto the bed beside her. "I'm not leaving you alone."

Maddie nodded, too tired to speak. As the room grew dark and the house below them fell back into silence, she held me close to her chest.

"I'm okay," she whispered again, as much to herself as to me.

But the truth was, she wasn't. Not really. And as her small body trembled beneath the covers, I wished more than anything that I could do more than just listen.

Chapter Sixteen

The morning light crept slowly into Maddie's room, casting pale stripes of gold across the faded white walls. The house was silent as she slowly stirred beneath her blankets. Every movement made her body ache, a dull throb reminding her of the night before.

She turned her head and saw Wyatt still asleep next to her, curled up on top of the blankets where he had stayed all night to keep her company. His chest rose and fell in steady rhythm, his face soft and peaceful in the pale morning light.

Maddie moved carefully so she wouldn't wake him. She clutched me close and took a deep breath. It was a school day. And school meant pretending everything was normal.

She swung her legs over the side of the bed and winced. She bit her lip to keep from making a sound. The ache deep inside her body was a heavy reminder of what had happened, one she wanted so badly to forget.

At her dresser, she picked out a pair of soft, loose-fitting leggings, the ones that didn't press too hard against her skin. Then she found her favorite Cinderella shirt, the light blue one with the Fairy Godmother on the front, wand raised high as she swirled silver and gold magic into the air. The sparkling letters underneath read, "Even Miracles Take a Little Time."

As she slipped the shirt over her head, she paused and stared down at the image. "I wish you were real," she whispered to the Fairy Godmother's painted smile. "I wish you could fix my daddy. Make him nice again. Make him stop hurting people."

Her voice trembled, and she swallowed hard. "Maybe if you waved your wand, he wouldn't drink anymore. Or yell. Or…" She didn't finish the sentence. Some wishes hurt too much to say out loud.

She tugged the shirt down gently, careful not to let the fabric brush too hard against the tender places on her back. It still hurt when she moved too quickly, so she learned to move slowly, gracefully, almost like a dancer trying not to disturb a sleeping giant.

At the small mirror above her dresser, Maddie brushed her hair and tied it back with a pale blue ribbon that matched Cinderella's gown. She looked at her reflection and tried to smile, but it felt thin and shaky. The girl staring back at her looked tired and older than seven, somehow.

But she also looked determined.

School was her escape. It was where she could read and sing and learn things that made her world bigger. And today, she would go there, even if it meant pretending everything was fine.

"Maddie," Wyatt's sleepy voice mumbled from behind her, his eyes still half closed. "You almost ready?"

"Yeah," she said softly. "Almost."

She tucked me gently under her arm, smoothing the wrinkles in my pink lace dress. "Come on, Jane," she whispered. "We've got a big day today."

Wyatt rubbed his eyes and helped her with her boots and backpack, then the two of them headed downstairs.

Their father was still passed out on the couch, snoring softly, and the stale smell of beer hung heavy in the air.

In the kitchen, the smell of toast and coffee drifted faintly from the counter. Mom wasn't there, not yet, but they could hear the faint hum of the bathroom fan and the soft clink of makeup bottles from down the hall.

"Do you think she's okay?" Maddie whispered.

Wyatt hesitated before answering. "She's trying to be," he said quietly.

A few minutes later, Mom appeared in the doorway. Her hair was freshly brushed and curled, and her eyes were ringed with carefully applied makeup. Maddie noticed how much foundation she'd used on the left side of her face, and how the bruising beneath her eye was still faintly visible, no matter how hard she tried to hide it.

"Good morning, babies," she said with a tired smile. "There's cereal on the counter."

Maddie ran to hug her waist, and Mom kissed the top of her head. For a moment, everything felt normal, like any other family morning before school. But as Mom poured her coffee and tucked a stray strand of hair behind her ear, Maddie could see the truth hiding just beneath the surface.

She didn't say anything. Neither did Wyatt. They all just pretended, because pretending was sometimes the only way to make it through the morning.

After breakfast, Wyatt zipped up his jacket and Maddie buttoned hers. They slipped quietly past the couch, where their father still lay unmoving, and stepped out into the cold morning.

Maddie stood with me clutched tightly against her chest, the crisp winter air stinging her cheeks. Her back ached and every step felt careful, but she lifted her chin and looked toward the road, searching for the familiar yellow bus.

And as she stood there in her Cinderella shirt, the Fairy Godmother's wand sparkling in the morning light, she whispered one last wish into the cold air.

"Please," she said softly, "make things better."

Chapter Seventeen

The long, cold winter melted slowly into spring, and before they knew it, the final bell of the school year had rung. Maddie could hardly believe how quickly the months had passed. There had been good days and bad ones, but today felt different. It was the beginning of summer. And tomorrow, they were going to Cape Cod.

She and Wyatt could barely contain their excitement as they ran up the driveway from the bus stop, backpacks bouncing, shoes splashing through the puddles left by an afternoon rain. Inside, the little house hummed with an unusual energy, the kind that came with getting ready to go somewhere special.

Suitcases were scattered across the living room, half-filled with swimsuits, beach towels, and clothes neatly folded into little stacks. Mom was in the kitchen, carefully labeling meals and tucking them into the refrigerator, one for each day they'd be gone. "I want to make sure your father has food while we're away," she said over her shoulder, writing Tuesday - Meatloaf in neat block letters on a strip of masking tape.

Their father sat slouched on the couch, cigarette dangling from his lips and a beer sweating in his hand. The familiar smell of Marlboros hung in the air. Wheel of Fortune played softly on the old television, the only sound he'd contributed all evening an occasional grunt at the contestants' guesses. He wasn't going on the trip. He never did.

Maddie didn't mind.

She had bigger things to think about.

In her room, she sat cross-legged on the floor beside the little suitcase she shared with Wyatt, holding me tightly in her arms. "We're going to have so much fun, Jane," she whispered, her blue eyes sparkling with excitement. "Papa's taking us to the beach, and I'm going to swim and pretend I'm a real mermaid." She lifted me into the air and twirled. "You'll see! The waves will splash around us, and we'll find seashells and maybe even a sand dollar."

She leaned closer, her voice dropping to a conspiratorial whisper. "And we're going to Martha's Vineyard, too. Mama says we're going to ride the flying horses carousel. Papa said it's really old, like, really old, and if I catch the brass ring, I can make a wish." She paused, pressing my cloth hands to her cheek. "I already know what I'm going to wish for."

Wyatt poked his head into the room, a bathing suit draped over his shoulder. "You better pack your sandals, Maddie. Mom says we're leaving right after breakfast."

"I already did," Maddie said proudly, holding up a pair of faded pink flip-flops.

"Good," Wyatt said, grinning. "I can't wait to go to the beach. Papa says he's bringing his kite."

The evening slipped by quickly in a whirl of last-minute packing and checklists. Mom double-checked bags, zipped up suitcases, and placed them neatly by the door. The fridge was lined with labeled meals, and the kitchen was clean and quiet. Through it all, their father barely looked up from his beer or his television. It didn't matter.

Tonight wasn't about him.

When the suitcases were ready and the house was calm again, Mom called them both into the living room. "All right, you two," she said softly, "it's bedtime. We've got a big day tomorrow."

Maddie and Wyatt brushed their teeth and climbed into their beds, giggling and whispering about all the things they would do; sandcastles and seashells, kites and carousel rides. Maddie placed me beside her pillow and tucked me in gently.

Mom came into the room a few minutes later. Her eyes looked tired, but her smile was warm. She pulled the blankets up to Maddie's chin and kissed her forehead softly. "I can't wait to watch you play in the ocean," she said.

"Me too," Maddie whispered sleepily. "I'm going to be a mermaid."

Mom chuckled quietly. "I don't doubt it." She kissed Wyatt's head too and whispered goodnight before turning out the light.

As the house settled into silence, Maddie hugged me close and let her thoughts drift to the salty air and crashing waves she would see tomorrow. She imagined the feeling of sand between her toes and the sun warming her face.

And as she drifted into dreams of seashells and flying horses, the pain of winter felt just a little farther away.

Chapter Eighteen

Morning came quickly, but Maddie was up before the sun. The moment her eyes fluttered open, her heart began to race, today was the day. Today they were going to Cape Cod.

She sprang out of bed, the soreness still lingering but overshadowed by her excitement. Wyatt stirred a few minutes later, rubbing the sleep from his eyes and grinning when he remembered what day it was. "We're going to the Cape!" he whispered, and Maddie nodded eagerly.

They hurried to get dressed, Maddie choosing her pink shorts and her favorite shirt with Ariel on the front, the perfect outfit for a future mermaid. Before heading downstairs, she carefully gathered me, Trisha, and Rabberta in her arms. "No one gets left behind," she whispered. "We're all going."

Downstairs, the smell of toast and eggs filled the kitchen. Mom was at the stove humming softly as she flipped breakfast on the old cast-iron pan. "Good morning, sleepyheads," she said warmly. "Eat up. We've got a long drive ahead."

Maddie and Wyatt gobbled down their breakfast, the excitement making them barely able to sit still. They checked their bags twice and carried them to the door where the old Caprice Classic was already cooling in the driveway. It was a big, faded blue car, "a boat," as Mom always called it, and it had been in the family for as long as Maddie could remember.

They piled in, the back seat piled high with suitcases, snacks, and beach towels. Maddie sat by the window, all of her friends lined up beside her, me in her lap, Rabberta tucked against her side, and Trisha strapped in with the seatbelt so she could "see" the view too.

As they pulled out of the driveway, Mom popped in her favorite cassette, Women of the '50s and '60s. The label on the tape was so worn from use that the song list had nearly rubbed off, but Maddie didn't need to read it. She knew every word by heart.

Soon, the car was filled with music and laughter. Maddie and Wyatt sang along to The Supremes and The Shirelles, their voices rising and falling with the cheerful melodies. Between songs, they played license plate bingo, searching the highway for cars from as many states as they could find.

"Vermont!" Maddie shouted.

"New York!" Wyatt added a minute later.

They played Ten Questions and an Answer, too — a game where one person picked something and the others had to guess what it was with only ten questions. Wyatt's answers were always animals. Maddie's were almost always Disney characters.

"Is it from a movie?" Wyatt asked.

"Yes," Maddie replied, grinning.

"Is it a princess?"

"Nope."

"Is it Sebastian?"

She laughed. "How did you guess that so fast?"

"It's always The Little Mermaid with you," he teased, nudging her shoulder.

The four-hour trip flew by faster than anyone expected. The music, the games, and the bubbling excitement made the time feel like a blink. Maddie pressed her nose to the window as the scenery changed from rolling Vermont hills to glimpses of coastline and salt marshes, her heart racing faster with every mile.

"Look!" she shouted as they turned down a familiar sandy road. "I see Papa's house!"

Before the Caprice Classic even came to a full stop, Papa was already at the gate. He must have been watching for them, because the moment the car pulled into the drive, he was there, waving and grinning from ear to ear.

"Welcome to Cape Cod!" he boomed as they climbed out of the car. His arms wrapped around Wyatt first, then Maddie, lifting her clean off the ground in a hug that made her giggle. He hugged Mom too, holding her tight for a moment longer, as if he could erase all the hard months behind them with one squeeze.

The salty breeze danced through Maddie's hair, carrying with it the sound of distant gulls and the promise of waves on the shore. She held me tight against her chest and looked up at the wide blue sky.

"We made it," she whispered to me, smiling so wide it hurt. "We're really here."

Chapter Nineteen

The next morning dawned bright and beautiful, the salty air drifting through the open windows of Papa's Cape Cod home. Maddie woke up with the sunlight streaming across her face and a smile already on her lips. Today was beach day.

She dressed quickly, slipping into her little bathing suit with seashell patterns and tugging a pair of shorts over it. I was tucked securely under her arm, of course, and Rabberta and Trisha were placed carefully on the bed to "guard the room" while she was gone. Wyatt was already bouncing with energy, chattering about all the crabs and shells he planned to find.

Mom packed a big canvas beach bag with towels, sunscreen, and snacks like peanut butter and jelly sandwiches wrapped in wax paper, and sleeves of peanut butter crackers stacked neatly in a container. "For when you two get hungry from all that swimming," she said with a smile, slipping a few napkins inside too.

Papa loaded the old beach chairs into the back of the car. "All right, mermaids and explorers," he said with a grin, "let's go find the ocean."

The short drive to the beach was filled with laughter and songs from the same well-loved cassette tape that had carried them all the way from Vermont. As soon as they stepped out of the car, the salty breeze rushed over them, and the rhythmic crash of waves filled the air. Maddie inhaled deeply, her heart fluttering with joy.

The sand was warm beneath her feet as they found a perfect spot near the shoreline. Papa and Mom spread out a blanket and set up their chairs while Maddie and Wyatt raced toward the water.

"Look, Jane!" Maddie said, holding me up to the sunlight as she knelt near the surf. "We're real mermaids now!" She twirled and danced at the water's edge, her feet splashing through the shallow waves. Then she knelt to collect seashells; pink, white, and soft shades of lavender and holding them up like treasure. Each one went carefully into her little sand pail.

Wyatt was a few feet away, crouched low and focused, carefully scooping up hermit crabs and tiny snails into a bucket. "Look at this one, Maddie!" he called out. "He's got a whole house on his back!"

"Hi, little crab!" Maddie giggled, leaning over the bucket. "Do you want to be part of my mermaid kingdom?"

The day drifted by in a golden blur of sunlight, laughter, and salty air. They built sandcastles that towered high, chased waves as they rolled in, and even buried Papa's feet in the sand while he pretended to be trapped.

When their stomachs rumbled, Mom called them over to the blanket. They munched on peanut butter and jelly sandwiches, sticky and sweet from the summer sun, and peanut butter crackers that crunched perfectly with every bite. "Best beach lunch ever," Wyatt declared with his mouth full, and Maddie giggled in agreement.

When the sun began to dip low in the sky, painting the water in shades of pink and gold, they returned to the house, tired and happy. The smell of Papa's cooking soon filled the air. It was his signature Cape dinner, grilled pork with smoky, homemade baked beans bubbling on the stove.

"Nothing says summer like this," Papa declared, handing out plates piled high with food.

The four of them ate together at the old picnic table in the backyard, the warm breeze tugging gently at Maddie's hair. She listened to the sound of seagulls in the distance and felt something she hadn't felt in a long time: safe.

That night, Maddie curled up on the cozy four-season porch that served as her room whenever they visited. The crickets chirped softly outside the windows, and a gentle sea breeze carried the faint scent of salt and sand into the room. She tucked me under her arm and pulled the blanket up to her chin, a contented sigh escaping her lips.

"This was the best day ever," she whispered into the darkness.

Her eyelids grew heavy, and before long, she drifted into a peaceful sleep, dreaming of seashells and mermaids, of kites dancing in salty winds, and of summer days that felt like they could last forever.

Chapter Twenty

Two mornings later, the Ryder family was up early, excitement buzzing through the house like sunshine. Today, they were going to Martha's Vineyard.

Papa drove them to Falmouth, where the Island Queen ferry waited at the dock. The big white boat gleamed in the sun, and gulls circled overhead, calling out as if to send them off. Maddie's heart beat fast with joy as she clutched me tightly, Wyatt bouncing beside her.

The salty breeze whipped through their hair as the ferry pulled away from the mainland. Maddie leaned against the rail, eyes wide, watching the waves sparkle like diamonds in the morning light. "Look, Jane," she whispered to me. "We're sailing to an island. Just like in a storybook."

Mom and Papa pointed out sailboats gliding by, and Wyatt counted them loudly, determined not to miss a single one. The ride only took about forty-five minutes, but to Maddie it felt like a grand adventure across the sea.

When they arrived at Oak Bluffs, the first stop was a little bakery tucked along a busy street. The windows steamed with the smell of sugar and cinnamon, and inside, the counters overflowed with pastries. Papa bought a box of fresh, golden apple fritters, bigger than Maddie's hand, glazed with sugar, warm and sticky inside.

"They're the best you'll ever have," Papa promised.

Maddie took a bite, her eyes widening in delight. The fritter was crisp at the edges, soft in the middle, full of cinnamon-sweet apples. "It's like magic," she whispered, cheeks full, and everyone laughed.

After their snack, they walked through the colorful streets, past gingerbread cottages painted like candy houses, until they reached the big red-and-white building Maddie had been waiting for: the Flying Horses Carousel.

It was beautiful! The oldest carousel she'd ever seen, the wooden horses shining with bright paint and golden manes. Music filled the air as the carousel spun, riders reaching out to grab brass rings from the dispenser as they whirled past.

Maddie's eyes sparkled. "I want to ride!"

"Of course you do," Mom said with a smile, buying tickets.

Wyatt helped Maddie up onto one of the tall painted horses, then climbed onto the one beside her. Papa and Mom stood at the rail, waving.

The carousel began to turn, faster and faster, music clanging from the old organ. Maddie laughed as the horse lifted and dipped beneath her. "I'm flying, Jane!" she shouted over the music. "Flying like the wind!"

Wyatt leaned out, stretching his arm toward the brass ring dispenser. He missed the first time, then tried again, determination etched on his face. On his third try, his fingers closed around something cool and heavy. When he looked, his eyes went wide.

"The golden ring!" he shouted, holding it high.

The ride slowed to a stop, and the attendant clapped. "Free ride for the one with the golden ring!"

Wyatt turned and pressed it into Maddie's hand. "You take it," he said firmly.

Maddie's eyes grew big. "But you won it."

"Yeah, but you've been dreaming about this since we got here. You should ride again."

She threw her arms around him in a quick hug. "Thank you, Wyatt!"

On her second ride, Maddie laughed so hard her cheeks hurt. She reached out for the rings, catching one after another, the salty air tangling in her hair. For a few shining minutes, she felt weightless, like a real princess, like the fairy tales she loved so much.

After the carousel, Papa suggested one more stop before they headed home. "We can't come all this way and not see the beach," he said with a wink.

They piled into a small shuttle and rode across the island to South Beach, where the Atlantic stretched out endlessly before them. The waves crashed against the shore, and the wind tugged playfully at Maddie's hair. She and Wyatt kicked off their shoes and raced along the sand, their laughter swept away by the ocean breeze. Maddie pretended she was a mermaid again, dipping her toes into the chilly surf.

On the way back, they stopped at a little bridge that Papa pointed out proudly. "That's Jaws Bridge," he said. "They filmed part of the movie Jaws here."

Wyatt's eyes went wide. "Really? The shark movie?"

"That's the one," Papa chuckled. "In the summer, people even jump off this bridge into the water below."

Maddie peered over the edge, the water sparkling beneath them. "Not today," she giggled, clutching me tighter. "Mermaids don't jump from bridges."

Papa laughed. "Not today, little mermaid. Not today."

By the time they caught the ferry back to Falmouth, Maddie's pockets were stuffed with shells, a ribboned brass ring token for keepsake, and her heart was light.

That night, as she curled up on the porch bed, she whispered to me, "Jane, today was the best day ever. I wish we could stay here forever."

And as the sea breeze drifted through the screens, carrying the scent of salt and summer, Maddie fell asleep dreaming of flying horses, golden rings, and mermaids beneath the bridge.

Chapter Twenty-One

The final morning of their Cape Cod vacation dawned bright and breezy, sunlight spilling through the windows of Papa's house and the salty air drifting in from the sea. Maddie woke with a mix of happiness and sadness. Happy for one more day of fun, sad that tomorrow they would have to leave.

"We have to make today the best day," she whispered to me as she got dressed. "The very best."

When she was ready, Maddie stepped out of the cozy porch where she'd been sleeping and walked into the main part of the house. The smell of something warm and familiar drifted through the air. Papa was already in the kitchen, humming to himself at the old gas stove, flipping his famous Mickey pancakes, the same ones he always made for special days.

"Good morning, sleepyheads!" he said cheerfully as Maddie and Wyatt came in, their hair still messy from sleep. "I made your favorite."

He slid a plate of golden pancakes in front of them, each one shaped like Mickey's smiling face with chocolate chip eyes. Maddie giggled when she saw the next plate.

"And this," Papa said proudly, "is my attempt at Donald Duck."

Wyatt tilted his head. "It looks more like Donald mixed with Goofy," he teased, and they all burst out laughing.

"Hey, art is open to interpretation," Papa said, grinning.

They devoured breakfast together, the warm pancakes soaked in maple syrup, laughter filling the kitchen. It was the perfect start to their last day, a memory that Maddie knew she'd hold onto for a very long time.

After breakfast, they packed up the beach bag one last time and piled into the car. The drive to the shore was filled with more laughter and singing along to Mom's favorite '50s and '60s cassette, the songs now so familiar they felt like part of the family.

The beach was already alive when they arrived, children chasing waves, gulls swooping overhead, the smell of salt and sunscreen thick in the warm air. Maddie slipped off her sandals the second her feet touched the sand and ran toward the water, twirling and laughing as the waves rolled around her ankles.

Wyatt helped Papa set up a bright red kite they'd brought with them. "You ready to fly this thing, champ?" Papa asked, handing him the spool.

"Ready!" Wyatt grinned.

The wind was perfect. Together, they launched the kite into the air, and Maddie squealed with delight as it soared higher and higher, the long tail fluttering like a ribbon against the brilliant blue sky.

"Look how high it's going!" she shouted, shielding her eyes from the sun.

"It's flying over the ocean!" Wyatt laughed, holding the string tight as the kite dipped and climbed in the sea breeze. Maddie took a turn too, feeling the pull of the wind through the string in her hands, like she was holding on to the sky itself.

After hours of playing in the waves and searching for seashells, Papa announced it was time for a special farewell dinner. They packed up their things and drove to Seafood Sam's, Papa's favorite little seafood restaurant on the Cape.

The smell of fried fish and saltwater filled the air as they walked inside. Maddie ordered her favorite, fish and chips, and savored every bite, the crispy coating crackling as she chewed. Papa slid a basket of golden onion rings across the table toward her.

"Here, mermaid," he said with a wink. "You can't come to Seafood Sam's and not share the onion rings."

Maddie giggled and dipped one into ketchup. "These are the best," she said between bites.

"Only the best for my girl," Papa replied, smiling.

After dinner, they made one last stop, back to the beach to say goodbye properly. The sun was dipping below the horizon, painting the sky with streaks of pink, orange, and violet. Papa pulled a small box of sparklers from his pocket, and Wyatt's eyes lit up.

"Really?" he asked.

"Really," Papa grinned.

They lit the sparklers one by one, the golden sparks hissing and dancing against the twilight sky. Maddie waved hers in big swirling circles, pretending it was a magic wand.

"Bippity boppity boo!" she sang, twirling in the sand. "I cast a spell for summer to stay forever!"

Wyatt laughed and waved his sparkler like a sword, and Mom snapped pictures as the two of them chased each other across the sand. Even Papa joined in, writing his name in glowing letters against the night.

When Maddie's sparkler finally burned down to nothing, she held the cool metal stick to her chest and sighed. "I hope the magic works," she whispered to me.

As they walked back up the beach, the waves gently lapping at the shore, Maddie looked over her shoulder one last time. The kite string, the onion rings, the sparkler spells, they were all tucked into her heart now, souvenirs of a week that had felt almost too good to be real.

And though she knew tomorrow they would have to leave, tonight the magic of Cape Cod still shimmered all around her in the sea breeze, the soft sand, and the love that wrapped around them like a warm blanket.

Chapter Twenty-Two

The summer days grew shorter, the air turning cooler in the evenings, and before they knew it, the Ryder house was buzzing with excitement for Wyatt's birthday party. Maddie had been helping Mom hang streamers and blow up balloons all morning, her little fingers sticky with tape. The smell of cake baking drifted through the house, and laughter echoed from the backyard as Wyatt's friends started to arrive.

Wyatt was beaming, racing around the yard with his friends, showing them the decorations and talking about the cake. Maddie followed close behind with me tucked under her arm, happy just to be part of the fun.

But Dad had company, too. A small group of his friends were scattered around the porch and lawn chairs, laughing too loudly and drinking from cans that clinked together. The sharp smell of beer hung in the air, and even though Maddie tried not to pay attention, she could feel her stomach twist the way it always did when they were around.

When it was time for presents, Wyatt sat proudly in front of everyone, grinning from ear to ear. He tore open colorful paper and lifted out his gifts, some clothes, a few books, and then the one that made his eyes light up: a brand-new street hockey set. Sticks, a net, and a bright orange ball, everything he'd wanted.

"Wow! Thanks!" he said, hugging Mom and Papa tight.

Dad took the box from him, pulling out the pieces and carrying them out to the backyard, where he began setting it all up. Wyatt bounced on his toes, practically vibrating with excitement, ready to play the first game with his friends.

But once the net was in place, Dad grabbed one of the sticks for himself, tossing another to one of his buddies. Before long, he and his friends had taken over the game, laughing and stumbling across the grass as they chased the ball.

"Here we go, boys!" Dad shouted, firing the ball toward the net while Wyatt and his friends stood off to the side.

The laughter from the adults grew louder as the kids watched in silence. Wyatt's face fell, his joy fading as quickly as it had come. One by one, his friends drifted over to the picnic bench and sat beside him, their excitement replaced with disappointment. Maddie's little heart ached as she saw her brother lower his head.

Papa noticed too. He walked over quietly and knelt beside Wyatt. "Hey, champ," he said softly. "Why aren't you playing with your new set?"

Wyatt shrugged, his voice small. "They're using it."

Papa's jaw tightened. He stood and strode toward Dad. "You've had your fun," he said evenly. "Let the kids play, it's Wyatt's birthday."

Dad snorted, waving him off. "Relax, old man. We're just having fun."

"This isn't your day," Papa said, his voice calm but unshakable. "It's your son's. And right now, he's sitting on a bench while you and your buddies act like teenagers."

Dad's smile faded, replaced with a scowl. "Don't tell me how to raise my kids," he snapped.

Papa's patience was gone. He grabbed Dad firmly by the arm and guided him toward the back door. "Then we're going to talk about it inside," he said sharply, unwilling to make a scene in front of the children.

The screen door slammed behind them, and for a few minutes, the backyard was silent except for the breeze rustling the party decorations. Then Papa came back out, his expression softer now.

"Alright, kids," he said with a smile. "Game's yours."

Wyatt's face lit up. He jumped from the bench and grabbed a stick, his friends following with cheers. Soon the backyard was filled with shouts of excitement as they darted back and forth, the orange ball clacking against sticks and skimming across the grass.

Maddie and I watched from the sidelines. "Go, Wyatt!" she shouted, pumping her fists in the air.

I waved too, playing along as the official cheerleader. "You can do it!" Maddie sang, her voice full of joy. "Score one for the birthday boy!"

Wyatt grinned at her between plays, and for the first time that afternoon, Maddie saw the happiness return to his eyes.

Later, as the sun began to dip lower, Mom came out of the kitchen carrying a cake that made everyone gasp. It was shaped like Optimus Prime, Wyatt's absolute favorite Transformer, bright blue and red frosting carefully piped into the details of the Autobot leader.

Wyatt's eyes widened. "You made this?" he asked, his voice full of awe.

Mom laughed. "Of course I did. Every hero needs a special cake."

They gathered around the picnic table, candles flickering in the breeze. Everyone sang "Happy Birthday" at the top of their lungs, and Wyatt beamed brighter than the candles themselves. He closed his eyes, made a wish, and blew them all out in one big breath.

"Best birthday ever," he whispered to Maddie as they shared a slice of cake.

When the sun dipped low and the last piece of cake was gone, Wyatt sat beside her on the porch steps, sweaty and smiling. "That hockey game was the best part," he said, licking frosting from his fingers.

Maddie hugged me tighter and smiled back. "You were amazing," she told him. "Best hockey player ever."

And though the day had started with disappointment, it ended with the kind of memory that would stick, not because of the presents or the cake, but because Papa had stepped in and made sure that Wyatt got to be a kid again.

Chapter Twenty-Three

The house smelled like Thanksgiving from the moment Maddie opened her eyes, warm and rich, the air heavy with the scent of turkey roasting and cinnamon apples simmering on the stove. The old wood stove creaked as it heated the house, wrapping everything in its cozy warmth.

Thanksgiving was one of Maddie's favorite holidays, not just because of the food, but because Papa and Grammy were coming. They came from two different sides of the family and always arrived in separate cars. To Maddie, that meant two hugs, two smiles, and two people who loved her in their own ways.

She ran down the stairs with me tucked under her arm, her little feet thumping on the wood. In the kitchen, Mom was bustling, apron tied around her waist. Wyatt sat at the table peeling potatoes, grumbling but doing his part.

"When are they coming?" Maddie asked eagerly.

"Soon," Mom said with a smile, glancing up from the mixing bowl. "You'll see their cars pull in."

Papa arrived first, his old truck rumbling up the driveway. Maddie flung the door open and ran straight into his arms before he even knocked.

"There's my girl," he said, spinning her once in the entryway. His coat smelled faintly of cold air and aftershave, a scent Maddie always associated with safety.

Grammy came next, pulling into the driveway in her little blue sedan. She stepped out with her pie dish carefully in her hands. Her hair was dyed dirty blonde, held in tight curls close to her head. She wore her favorite soft sweater, and as soon as she stepped inside, the smell of lilacs and sugar cookies filled the air.

"Oh my sweet Maddie," Grammy said as Maddie ran to her. She bent down, set the pie aside, and pulled Maddie into her soft arms. "I missed you so much."

"I missed you too, Grammy," Maddie whispered, holding on tight.

Soon, more of Dad's family filled the house. Cigarette smoke mingled with the smell of turkey. Laughter and loud conversations bounced off the walls. Dad was already drinking, his voice rising above the chatter.

But for a while, Maddie focused on the good. The mismatched plates on the table looked beautiful to her. The turkey was golden, the mashed potatoes fluffy, and Papa made his famous gravy. Wyatt teased her for stealing the biggest roll. Grammy helped her scoop cranberry sauce.

The laughter at the table almost felt normal. But beneath it all, Maddie could sense the shadows.

Grammy's soft, wrinkled hands trembled when Dad's voice grew sharp. She flinched at certain tones, tones Maddie knew too well. She didn't understand everything then, but later she would. Grammy wasn't just kind. She was someone who had lived through her own storms.

When Dad was a boy, Grampy, her husband, had been an alcoholic. He'd hurt Grammy and hurt Dad. Violence had lived in their home the way it now lived in Maddie's. Dad's cruelty hadn't been born from nowhere. It had been learned, passed down like an unwanted, ugly family heirloom.

Knowing that later wouldn't excuse what he did, but it helped Maddie understand the shape of the pain.

As the grown-ups drank and talked, Maddie stayed close to Papa and Grammy. Papa slipped her an extra slice of pie, Grammy smoothed her hair and told her she was loved. For a while, she felt safe.

Later that evening, after the dishes were washed and most of the family had drifted into the living room, Papa and Grammy stood near the kitchen window, voices low. Maddie couldn't hear every word from the hallway, but their tone was soft and heavy with worry.

"He's turning into his father," Grammy whispered, her voice trembling. "I tried to protect him. God knows I did... but it grew in him anyway."

Papa leaned against the counter, his jaw tight. "I see it," he said quietly. "And the kids... they see it too."

Grammy clutched the counter, blinking back tears. "I'm scared for them. I can see it in their little faces. They're living through the same hell I did."

Papa's voice hardened, steady and sure. "They've got me and you. And their mom. We're not going to let what happened to you and him keep happening to those kids. The chain ends here."

Grammy nodded slowly, her eyes glistening. "I hope so. I really hope so."

Papa glanced toward the stairs, toward Maddie's room, where soft giggles floated down the hallway. "No," he said firmly. "I know so."

When Maddie finally climbed into bed with me that night, the house was still noisy downstairs, but she held onto the good parts of the day, the smell of turkey, Grammy's warm hug, Papa's laugh, and the feeling of being loved by at least two people who truly cared.

She whispered into the quiet, "Someday it'll be different."

And from my place in her arms, I felt it too.
The house carried the weight of old pain, but that night, I also felt something stronger! the quiet flicker of hope beginning to take root.

Chapter Twenty-Four

The fall months slipped quietly into winter, the bright leaves giving way to frosty mornings and snow-dusted afternoons. School had started again, and while Maddie tried her best, it was still hard. She loved reading stories and singing in music class, and she always did well when she could use her imagination. But math still tangled her up, and sometimes the noise and chatter of the classroom made her feel small.

She had a few friends, girls who would sit with her at lunch or play jump rope with her at recess, but most days, she still felt like she didn't quite fit in. Still, as December crept closer, Maddie grew more and more excited. It was almost her birthday, and she wanted this one to be special.

Mom helped her write invitations in her careful, looping handwriting and handed them out at school. Maddie invited all the girls in her class, even Anna, hoping maybe, just maybe, they could start fresh and have fun together.

The day of the party, the Ryder house was warm and cheerful, filled with the smell of cake baking and hot chocolate simmering on the stove. Paper streamers in shades of purple and gold hung from the walls, and a big Happy Birthday Maddie! banner stretched across the living room. Maddie wore her favorite sparkly pink dress and carried me proudly in her arms, her heart beating with excitement as the doorbell rang.

One by one, the girls from her class came inside, stamping snow from their boots and handing her brightly wrapped presents with bows and ribbons. "Happy birthday, Maddie!" they chirped, smiling sweetly. Maddie's heart swelled, maybe this would be the birthday where she really felt like she belonged.

For a while, everything was perfect. They played musical chairs, passed around balloon animals, and laughed as they shared snacks and stories. Maddie felt happy, like maybe she really was part of the group.

But then, when the adults stepped into the kitchen to talk, Anna spoke up. "Let's play princesses," she suggested, twirling a strand of her glossy dark hair around her finger.

Maddie's eyes lit up. "I love princesses! Can I be Jasmine?"

Anna smiled, but it didn't quite reach her eyes. "Actually," she said, glancing at the other girls, "we already decided you can be the servant. You know, the one who does everything for the princesses."

The other girls giggled and nodded. "Yeah, Maddie, that's a really important part," one of them added.

Maddie hesitated. "Oh… okay." Her chest felt tight, but she wanted them to like her, so she agreed.

"Great!" Anna said brightly. "Then your first job is to go into the guest room and clean it up. Make sure it's spotless before you come back."

So Maddie did. She carried a small dust rag from the kitchen and went into the quiet guest room. It wasn't even messy, just a few things out of place, but she straightened the pillows and folded the throw blanket neatly, doing what they said.

From the hallway, she could hear the other girls laughing and playing with her new toys.

She peeked around the doorframe quietly and watched as they unwrapped her presents from the fresh packaging and played pretend without her. Their giggles were drifting through the air like tiny daggers. Tears pricked her eyes. She was supposed to be happy today. She was supposed to feel special. But instead, she felt invisible, a misfit at her own birthday party.

"Maybe they'll call me soon," she whispered to me, holding me tight against her chest. But they didn't.

Eventually, Mom's cheerful voice called from the kitchen, "Cake time!" and the girls all hurried to the table. Maddie wiped her eyes quickly and followed them, forcing a smile as Mom brought out the cake.

It was beautiful, an Aladdin cake, decorated with blue and gold frosting, and a tiny edible picture of Aladdin and Jasmine on the magic carpet. Maddie gasped when she saw it. "It's perfect," she whispered. Aladdin was her favorite movie that year, and she had dreamed about this cake for weeks.

As Mom began cutting slices, Anna leaned close. "I want the piece with Princess Jasmine," she said.

Maddie hesitated. "That's the one I wanted…" she murmured, her voice small.

Anna shrugged and lowered her voice. "Well, I'm the guest. Guests should get what they want. It's rude not to share, Maddie."

The words stung. Maddie's hands fidgeted in her lap. Slowly, she nodded. "Okay. You can have it."

Anna smiled smugly as Mom handed her the piece. Maddie watched it go, her heart aching. She took a different slice and sat quietly while everyone sang "Happy Birthday."

She blew out the candles, her wish unspoken but heavy in her heart: I wish I didn't always feel so different. I wish I could be the princess too.

And though she smiled for the pictures and said thank you for the presents, deep down, Maddie felt lonelier than ever. Even on her special day, the one meant to celebrate her, she felt like she didn't quite belong.

When the last guest had left and the house grew quiet again, Papa patted the spot next to him on the couch. "Come here, birthday girl," he said gently.

Maddie climbed into his lap, curling up against his chest as he wrapped his arms around her. "Did you have a good birthday?" he asked softly.

Maddie nodded, though her voice was small. "It was okay."

Papa didn't press her. Instead, he reached into a small gift bag by his feet. "I have a few things for my favorite girl," he said with a smile. Inside was a soft, shimmery mermaid dress, the fabric sparkling like scales in the light.

Maddie's eyes lit up. "For me?"

"For you," Papa said. "I thought you might want to wear it to school on your birthday week. Every mermaid princess needs a special dress."

"It's beautiful," she whispered, hugging it tight.

"And," Papa added, pulling out a small stack of books, "these are for the smartest third grader I know."

Maddie read the title aloud, her eyes widening. "The Boxcar Children!"

Maddie beamed, holding the books close. Then she snuggled deeper into Papa's lap as he opened one of her favorite old storybook, the same orange-bound anthology he'd read from so many times before. His deep, steady voice filled the room as he read aloud, and the world outside seemed to melt away.

By the time he finished the story, Maddie's eyes were heavy and her heart felt a little lighter. She hugged Papa tight before bed, whispering, "Thank you, Papa. For everything."

And as she drifted off to sleep that night, her mermaid dress folded neatly on her chair and The Boxcar Children stacked on her nightstand, she felt something warm and certain: even when the world made her feel small, she was deeply loved.

Chapter Twenty-Five

The morning of Maddie's first school day after her birthday dawned with pale winter light spilling across her little room. She slipped into the beautiful mermaid dress Papa had given her, the shimmery fabric glistening like ocean waves in the sunlight. It swished softly around her knees as she spun in front of the mirror, holding me close.

"Do I look like a real mermaid, Jane?" she asked, twirling once more.

You look like the most magical mermaid there ever was, I thought, watching her smile widen.

When she arrived at school, heads turned almost immediately. "Wow, Maddie!" one girl gasped as she walked into the classroom. "That dress is so pretty!"

"I love it!" another chimed in. "It looks just like Ariel's!"

Maddie's heart soared. She'd never felt like the center of good attention before, and now, here she was, her classmates smiling at her instead of teasing. For once, she felt like she belonged.

At recess, as she sat swinging on the playground, a girl with curly brown hair and a bright green coat came up beside her. "Hi," she said shyly. "I'm Breanna."

"Hi," Maddie said, smiling.

"I really love your dress," Breanna said. "The Little Mermaid is my favorite movie."

Maddie's eyes lit up. "Mine too! I sing 'Part of Your World' all the time."

Breanna giggled. "Me too! My mom says I should be on Broadway."

The two girls dissolved into laughter, and just like that, something shifted. It wasn't just small talk. It was the beginning of a real friendship. They spent the rest of recess talking about their favorite songs, drawing mermaids in the snow with their boots, and promising to sit together at lunch.

Later that afternoon, as Maddie gathered her books before math class, she heard a voice behind her. "Hey, Maddie," said Jake, a boy from her class with sandy hair cut in a bowl cut, and freckles who was known for being funny and kind.

Maddie turned, clutching her books. "Hi, Jake."

He smiled. "I just wanted to say… you look really cute today."

Her cheeks turned bright pink. "Oh… thank you," she whispered, smiling shyly.

For the rest of the day, Maddie couldn't stop sneaking glances at him from across the room. Every time he smiled or raised his hand, her heart did a tiny flip. It was confusing and exciting all at once, something new and wonderful she didn't quite have words for.

But not everyone was happy about it. At recess the next day, Anna stomped across the playground toward Maddie, her eyes narrowed. "I saw you looking at Jake," she hissed. "He's mine. Why would he ever want someone like you?"

The words landed like stones in Maddie's chest. She opened her mouth but no sound came out.

Before she could say anything, Breanna stepped between them, her hands on her hips. "Because Maddie is a really nice person," she said firmly. "And nice people are way better than mean ones."

Anna's face flushed bright red. "Whatever," she muttered, spinning on her heel and storming off with a huff.

Maddie stared at Breanna, eyes wide. "Thank you," she whispered.

Breanna smiled. "That's what friends do."

And as they walked back toward the swings together, Maddie felt something warm and new bloom inside her chest. For the first time in a long time, she wasn't just surviving school, she was belonging. She had a real friend by her side… and maybe, just maybe, the beginnings of a first crush too.

Chapter Twenty-Six

The first snow of December had dusted the ground in a soft white blanket, and by the time Friday afternoon arrived, the Ryder house felt alive with excitement. Maddie and Wyatt climbed off the school bus, cheeks rosy from the cold and boots crunching in the snow. As they pushed open the front door, a wave of warmth and cinnamon-scented air greeted them, and so did a sight that made Maddie's heart leap.

"Mom! You're home early!" Wyatt shouted, dropping his backpack by the door.

"I sure am," Mom said with a smile, standing beside a pile of boxes of Christmas ornaments and decorations she had pulled up from the basement. On the table sat an old metal hand saw, its wooden handle worn smooth from years of use. Maddie's eyes sparkled the moment she saw it.

"Does that mean…?" she began, hardly able to contain her excitement.

Mom laughed. "That's right. We're going tree hunting!"

It was one of Maddie's favorite traditions since moving to Vermont, heading into the woods behind their house to find the perfect Christmas tree. They were lucky to have so many evergreens growing nearby, and it saved them from spending money they didn't have.

"Go bundle up!" Mom said. "It's cold out there."

In minutes, Maddie and Wyatt were zipped into their puffy winter coats, scarves wrapped snugly around their necks, hats tugged over their ears, and mittens pulled tight. Maddie grabbed me too, no adventure was complete without her favorite companion.

They crunched through the snow into the woods, their breath puffing little clouds in the crisp air. "Sleigh bells ring, are you listening…" Maddie began to sing softly.

Wyatt joined in, and soon their voices danced through the trees: "Walking in a winter wonderland!"

"Look!" Wyatt shouted suddenly, pointing to a towering evergreen a little ways ahead. "That one's perfect!"

It was beautiful, full and green, with branches that swept gracefully toward the snow. But as they stood beneath it, they realized it was far too tall.

"It's bigger than the whole living room," Mom laughed.

Maddie grinned. "If only we lived in a castle! Then it would fit!"

They all burst out laughing before continuing deeper into the woods. Finally, Wyatt spotted another tree — smaller but still lovely, with strong branches and a perfect shape.

"This one," Maddie said softly. "It's just right."

"Just right," Mom agreed.

With careful teamwork, Mom and Wyatt used the saw to cut it down, the crisp scent of pine filling the air as it tipped gently into the snow. Together, they dragged it back toward the house, laughing as the branches caught on their boots and snow sprinkled down on their hats.

Back inside, the house buzzed with warmth and anticipation. They propped the tree up in the stand near the big picture window and stepped back to admire it. It wasn't fancy, but it was theirs, and that made it perfect.

"Lights first!" Mom said, plugging in the old twinkle lights that had been used for as long as Maddie could remember. They wound them carefully around the branches, filling the tree with a soft golden glow.

Then came the ornaments, a delightful mix of shapes, colors, and memories. Some were glass balls, chipped from years of use. Others were handmade treasures from school projects: popsicle-stick stars, glitter-covered snowflakes, and cotton-ball snowmen with crooked smiles.

"Here's the one you made in kindergarten," Mom said, holding up a paper angel with Maddie's tiny handprint on the back. Maddie giggled and hung it near the middle of the tree.

Her favorite part came last, setting up the old wooden manger on the small table beside the tree. Its paint had faded over time, but the little ceramic figures of Mary, Joseph, baby Jesus, the wise men, and the animals were still beautiful to Maddie.

"This is my favorite part," she whispered to me, carefully placing the baby Jesus figure into the manger.

She would spend hours playing with it, sometimes reenacting the nativity story she'd heard so many times, other times inventing her own stories for the figures. To Maddie, it was more than a decoration, it was a dollhouse filled with magic and wonder.

By the time they finished, the tree sparkled softly in the fading light, casting a warm glow across the room. Maddie sighed happily and curled up on the couch, staring at the twinkling lights. "It's perfect," she whispered.

But just as the house settled into a peaceful rhythm, the front door swung open. Dad walked in and he wasn't alone. A group of his cousins and friends stumbled in behind him, laughing loudly, the smell of alcohol clinging to their coats. Several of them had brought their children, who barreled noisily into the living room.

Mom froze, her smile faltering. She clearly hadn't been expecting company.

The cozy, peaceful evening they had planned shifted in an instant.

Chapter Twenty-Seven

The Ryder house was warm and glowing, the scent of fresh pine still hanging in the air from the tree they had brought home. But the mood shifted the moment Dad and his friends and family piled into the living room. They dropped onto the couch and chairs, laughing too loudly, cracking open beer after beer, and soon the sharp, skunky smell of marijuana filled the air. Their voices grew rough and slurred as the night went on.

Mom sighed quietly. She had planned a peaceful evening of baking sugar cookies with Maddie and Wyatt, but now she had more children to watch, the cousins. There were the twins, Karla and Kallie, who were Maddie's age, and Aaron, who was Wyatt's age.

"Well," Mom said gently, forcing a smile, "I guess we'll just have a bigger cookie party!"

She cleared off the kitchen table and set up a spot for each child with a wooden rolling pin, a little pile of dough, and shiny metal cookie cutters shaped like Christmas trees, Santa Claus, stars, and reindeer. Maddie pressed the cutters into the soft dough with delight, carefully lifting each cookie shape onto the baking sheet.

Karla and Kallie giggled as they worked, showing Maddie the ones they made. "This one looks like Santa ate too many cookies!" Kallie said, holding up a lopsided Santa shape.

Mom laughed. "That's okay. Even Santa deserves extra cookies."

While the cookies baked, Mom set out bowls of colorful sprinkles and sugar crystals, along with dishes of red, green, and white frosting and dull butter knives for spreading. She popped a cassette into the old tape player, and soon Raffi's cheerful voice filled the kitchen, singing Christmas classics.

The kids sang along as they decorated, their laughter rising above the muffled noise from the living room. For a little while, everything felt normal, even magical.

When the cookies cooled, Maddie carefully chose one she had decorated herself. A little Christmas tree covered in red sprinkles and green icing and tiptoed into the living room where Dad sat slouched on the couch with a beer in his hand.

"Daddy?" she said softly. "I made this one for you."

He blinked down at the cookie, and for a moment, the harshness melted from his face. "Thanks, kiddo," he said, taking it from her. "It's beautiful. You did a good job."

Maddie's chest swelled with warmth. It wasn't often she heard kind words from him.

Karla and Kallie soon followed, carrying their own plates of cookies for their dad. But his reaction was nothing like Maddie's father's. He laughed coldly and waved them away.

"We're gonna leave some for Santa," Karla said, still smiling hopefully.

"There's no point," their father slurred, leaning back in his chair. "Ain't gonna be no Santa this year. I ran him over with my truck."

The words hit like a punch. Karla's smile fell, and Kallie's lower lip trembled. "W-what?"

"No Santa," he said again, chuckling cruelly. "Guess you're outta luck."

Tears filled the twins' eyes. "That's not true!" Kallie cried, her voice breaking. Maddie felt her own throat tighten, tears spilling over as she hugged Rabberta to her chest. "Santa is real!" she sobbed.

The sound of crying carried through the room. Maddie's dad looked up sharply, his face darkening. "What did you just say to them?" he demanded, his voice like thunder.

The man shrugged. "Just telling them the truth."

That was the last straw. Maddie's dad stood up so quickly his beer tipped over. In two strides, he was across the room. "You don't ever talk to kids like that!" he roared, grabbing the man by the collar.

Before anyone could react, he dragged him through the front door and out into the cold night. Maddie and the kids crowded near the window, eyes wide. A shout split the air, followed by a loud crack as Maddie's dad punched him, sending him sprawling down the icy driveway.

The man groaned, clutching his face as he scrambled to his feet. The night was filled with yelling, slurred words and curses, and Maddie felt her chest tighten with fear.

The twins clung to each other, sobbing, and Wyatt wrapped an arm around them, his jaw set tight.

Inside, Mom moved quickly, her face pale but calm. "Alright, everyone," she said softly, ushering the children back toward the kitchen. "Let's go pick out the best cookies to leave for Santa. I think he'd like that."

Maddie nodded, wiping her tears, but the magic had dimmed. The sparkling lights on the Christmas tree still glowed in the corner, but the sound of angry voices outside made them feel colder somehow.

And though the cookies were sweet and the house smelled like cinnamon and sugar, a shadow hung over the night, one Maddie was too young to name, but old enough to feel deep in her heart.

Chapter Twenty-Eight

The house grew quieter after the fight in the driveway. One by one, Dad's cousins and friends drifted out into the cold night, some laughing, some muttering under their breath. The door slammed behind the last of them, leaving the Ryder home wrapped in an uneasy silence. The only sounds were the faint ticking of the kitchen clock and the soft hum of the refrigerator.

Maddie sat on the floor of her room upstairs, playing gently with me and Rabberta, trying to lose herself in a world of make-believe. But the muffled sound of voices downstairs kept pulling her back.

"Why would you invite that many people without telling me?" Mom's voice was tired, trembling just a little.

"They're family," Dad snapped back. "What's the big deal?"

"The big deal is you were drinking all night, the house was full of people I wasn't prepared for, and you scared the kids!"

"They're fine," he slurred. "You always make such a big deal out of nothing."

"It's not nothing," Mom said, her voice rising now. "You ruined what was supposed to be a peaceful night for them."

The words hit something raw in him. His tone changed harsher, darker. "You think you're so perfect, don't you?"

Maddie clutched me tighter, her stomach knotting. This was how it always started with sharp words, sharper tones. Then, suddenly, the sounds changed. Heavy footsteps. A crash. The slam of a cupboard door.

Then came running. Fast, thundering footsteps up the stairs. Maddie froze. A second later, there was a loud slam and the distinct sound of a lock clicking into place.

Wyatt.

Maddie crept to her bedroom door and turned the knob just enough to peek into the hallway. Wyatt's bedroom door was closed tight, and Dad was stumbling up the stairs after him, rage twisting his face.

"Open the fucking door, Wyatt!" he roared, pounding his fists against the wood. The sound shook the hallway, echoing like thunder. "I said OPEN IT!"

"Leave me alone!" Wyatt shouted from the other side, his voice cracking. "Just leave me alone!"

"Don't you tell me what to do in my own house!" Dad bellowed, slamming his fists harder, each hit making Maddie flinch.

Then, as suddenly as he'd charged up, he stumbled back down the stairs. For a moment, there was silence. A silence so heavy Maddie could hear her own heartbeat.

It didn't last.

The next sound was the metallic scrape of something being dragged across the wall. Then the heavy clank of boots on the stairs. Dad reappeared, a crowbar clutched in his hand, his eyes glassy and unfocused.

Maddie's breath caught in her chest. He raised the crowbar and slammed it against Wyatt's door. Once. Twice. Each blow rattled the frame and made the walls shake.

"OPEN THE DAMN DOOR!" he screamed. "I'll break it down if I have to!"

Maddie's hands trembled. She stepped into the doorway, fear gripping her from the inside out.

Then Mom appeared, racing up the stairs, her face pale and her eyes wide. "Stop it!" she yelled, grabbing his arm. "STOP!"

"Stay out of this!" he shouted, yanking away and pushing her back.

"Enough!" Mom screamed, stepping between him and the door. "You're scaring them!"

For a long moment, everything stood still, the hallway thick with tension, the air heavy with fear. Dad's chest heaved, the crowbar still clutched tightly in his hand.

Then his eyes shifted. They landed on Maddie. She was terrified, peeking out of her bedroom door.

"Go back in your room!" Mom shouted, her voice breaking. "Maddie, now! Shut the door and lock it!"

Maddie's breath came fast and shallow. She stumbled backward into her room, her hands shaking as she turned the lock and pressed her back against the door. I was clutched tightly in her arms, her heartbeat hammering against my fabric chest.

Down the hall, the sound of shouting carried on. Wood splintered under the force of the crowbar, and Wyatt's muffled cries bled through the noise. Maddie covered her ears and rocked on the floor, whispering over and over, "Please stop... please stop..."

The house that had been so full of Christmas warmth just hours before now felt cold and broken, the twinkling lights downstairs casting long, trembling shadows up the stairwell. And as the night dragged on, the magic of the season felt a million miles away.

Chapter Twenty-Nine

The shouting eventually faded into silence. The banging stopped. Somewhere downstairs, a door slammed, followed by heavy, uneven footsteps pacing the floor. And then, at last, the house grew still.

Maddie waited a long time. Long enough for her breathing to slow and the fear in her chest to settle into a heavy ache. The glow from the Christmas tree downstairs still flickered faintly against the hallway wall, casting a soft, trembling light under her door.

Quietly, she turned the lock and eased her door open. The hallway was empty now, the air cold and heavy. She padded softly down the hall, clutching me and Rabberta tight against her chest.

"Wyatt?" she whispered as she tapped gently on his door.

There was a pause, then the sound of shuffling feet. The door opened a crack, and Wyatt's tired, red-rimmed eyes peered out. "Maddie?"

Without a word, she slipped inside and closed the door behind her. Wyatt's room was dim, lit only by the faint glow of moonlight through the window. He climbed back into bed, curling up under his blanket, his face streaked with dried tears.

Maddie climbed in beside him, wrapping her small arms around his shoulders. "I'm here," she whispered.

Wyatt let out a shaky breath and leaned into her. "I'm okay," he murmured, but his voice cracked, betraying the pain he was trying so hard to hide.

"I know," Maddie whispered back. "I am too."

They held each other in the quiet, neither saying much after that. Words weren't needed. The closeness was enough. Maddie tucked Rabberta and Trisha between them, their soft faces watching over the two siblings as they slowly drifted into an exhausted, dreamless sleep.

As they slept, the Night Council gathered once more. Rabberta, pink and floppy with googly eyes that glimmered faintly in the moonlight, perched herself at the foot of the bed. Trisha, calm and motherly, sat by Wyatt's side. And I, Jane, took my place near Maddie's heart.

"They've been through so much," Rabberta whispered.

"Too much," Trisha agreed softly. "But they still have each other."

"And us," I added. "We'll keep watch tonight."

And we did. As the house creaked and sighed in the cold night, we stayed awake, silent sentinels guarding the children we loved. No more shouting. No more pounding fists. Just the soft rise and fall of their breathing and the faint hum of wind against the window.

When morning finally came, pale sunlight crept across the floorboards. The house was still, almost peaceful, as if the horrors of the night before were nothing but a terrible dream.

Downstairs, a knock came at the front door, firm and familiar. Wyatt stirred, rubbing his eyes, and Maddie sat up slowly, her hair tangled from sleep.

Through the thin walls, they heard Mom's voice, softer and warmer than it had been in days. "Dad... you're here."

A deeper, comforting voice answered. "Of course I am. It's Christmas."

Maddie's eyes lit up. "Papa's here!" she whispered, scrambling out of bed.

The night had been long and dark, but with the morning came hope. The steady, loving presence of the man who always made them feel safe.

Chapter Thirty

Christmas Eve arrived with the soft hush of falling snow blanketing the Vermont woods. The Ryder house glowed with the golden light of the tree, the scent of pine and sugar cookies still lingering in the air. Maddie and Wyatt spent the afternoon helping Mom finish wrapping gifts and sneaking peeks under the tree, their excitement bubbling higher with every passing hour.

As the sky darkened, Mom put a worn VHS tape into the old VCR, and the familiar jingle filled the living room: "Rudolph the Red-Nosed Reindeer…" Maddie snuggled into the couch beside Wyatt, holding me close as the old claymation classic flickered across the screen.

She watched Rudolph's nose glow bright red as the other reindeer laughed at him and Hermie the elf dreamed of being a dentist instead of making toys. Her heart tightened. She knew that feeling of being different, of not quite fitting in.

"I feel like them sometimes," she whispered softly into my fabric ear. "Like I don't belong."

But just like Rudolph and Hermie, Maddie held onto hope that maybe, just maybe, being different could be something special.

Dad was in his usual spot on the couch, a cigarette dangling from his fingers as he stared at the TV. He didn't say much, just exhaled long streams of smoke that curled toward the ceiling.

When the movie ended, Maddie and Wyatt scampered into the kitchen. "We have to get Santa's snack ready!" Wyatt said with a grin.

They carefully arranged a plate with the sugar cookies they'd baked, choosing the best ones for Santa. Maddie added a glass of milk and then ran to the fridge for one more thing.

"What are those for?" Wyatt asked as she placed a few carrots next to the cookies.

"For the reindeer," Maddie said matter-of-factly. "They do all the flying so they deserve a treat too."

Mom smiled softly from the doorway. "That's very thoughtful, sweetheart."

When the plate was set and placed by the tree, the house quieted. Snow continued to fall outside, blanketing the night in peaceful stillness. It was time for their favorite Christmas Eve tradition.

Papa settled into his chair with a familiar old book in his hands. "Alright, you two," he said with a twinkle in his eye. "Gather 'round. You know what night it is."

Maddie climbed into Mom's lap on the couch, curling up against her chest. Her mother's arms wrapped around her, warm and comforting, and she smelled faintly of Passion perfume. This same scent Maddie always associated with comfort, and home. Wyatt sprawled on the rug near Papa's feet, eyes bright with anticipation.

Papa opened the book, his voice deep and steady as he began:

"'Twas the night before Christmas, when all through the house,
Not a creature was stirring, not even a mouse…"

The familiar words wrapped around them like a soft blanket. Maddie closed her eyes and listened, her heart swelling with warmth. For a little while, the fear and sadness of nights past felt far away.

When Papa finished the story, he closed the book with a gentle thump and smiled. "Now, I have a little surprise for you both before bed," he said, reaching behind his chair.

He handed Wyatt a rectangular box wrapped in red paper. "For my favorite builder," Papa said with a grin. Wyatt tore it open and gasped. "K'NEX! Thanks, Papa!" He threw his arms around him, already talking about all the things he was going to build.

Then Papa turned to Maddie and handed her a larger box, carefully wrapped package tied with a golden ribbon. Maddie's hands trembled as she opened it. Inside was a beautifully crafted doll swing, made of smooth wood and painted pale pink.

"I made it just for you," Papa said softly. "I thought Jane and her friends might like a new ride."

Maddie's eyes filled with happy tears. "It's perfect, Papa," she whispered, hugging him tightly. "Thank you."

She carried the swing upstairs and placed it carefully by her bed. Rabberta hopped in first, her floppy pink ears hanging over the sides. Trisha and I joined next, and Maddie gave the swing a gentle push. "Hold on tight," she giggled. "It's time to fly."

A few minutes later, Mom and Papa came upstairs. They tucked Maddie in beneath her quilt, Papa kissing her forehead gently. "Merry Christmas, little mermaid," he whispered.

"Merry Christmas, Papa," she murmured, her eyelids heavy with sleep.

As the soft glow of the Christmas tree lights flickered from the living room below, Maddie drifted off into dreams filled with reindeer and magic sleigh rides, with Jane and Rabberta soaring through the snowy sky. And for the first time in a long time, her heart felt light.

Chapter Thirty-One

The house was still and silent in the soft hours before dawn. The tree's golden lights glowed gently against the dark picture window, casting dancing shadows across the living room walls. Outside, the world was hushed under a blanket of snow, the sky still deep indigo.

Maddie crept softly down the stairs, Jane tucked safely in her arms. Her bare feet made no sound on the worn wooden steps as she tiptoed toward the tree. She stopped a few feet away, her breath catching.

It was beautiful, more beautiful than she had remembered from the night before. The twinkling lights reflected in the glass ornaments, and the paper stars she and Wyatt had made in school swayed gently on the branches. Beneath the tree, packages in red and gold wrapping paper waited patiently to be opened.

She sat cross-legged on the floor, just staring at it all, feeling something warm flicker in her chest.

A soft rustle behind her made her turn. Papa was stirring in the recliner, where he had fallen asleep the night before. He blinked and smiled when he saw her.

"Morning, early bird," he whispered.

"Morning, Papa," Maddie whispered back.

"Couldn't sleep?"

She shook her head. "I wanted to see the tree before everyone woke up."

Papa patted his lap. "Come here, little mermaid."

Maddie climbed up and nestled against him, and for a moment everything felt safe. His arms wrapped around her, warm and familiar, but as he shifted to hug her tighter, Maddie gasped softly.

Papa immediately froze. "Hey… what's wrong?"

"It's nothing," Maddie mumbled, trying to shrug it off. "I'm fine."

Papa's brow furrowed. "Did I hurt you?"

She hesitated. "No… not you."

There was a long pause. Papa's voice was gentle but steady, the same tone he had used when helping frightened children in his years on the force. "Maddie," he said quietly, "you can tell me the truth. Did someone hurt you?"

Her lip trembled, and her eyes welled with tears. "I… I shouldn't have made him mad," she whispered.

Papa's heart clenched. "Who, sweetheart?"

Her small voice cracked. "Daddy."

The word hung heavy in the air. Papa's arms remained around her, strong and steady but never pressing. "What did he do?" he asked softly.

At first, the words came in broken pieces. Small details about hitting and nights filled with shouting and fear. But once she started, Maddie couldn't stop. It was like a dam breaking. Everything she had held inside, all the fear, confusion, and shame just spilled out in sobs and sentences.

She told him about the times he had hurt her and Wyatt. How he hit them when he was angry. How he hurt Mom too. And then, in a trembling voice, she shared something that made Papa's chest tighten even more, how sometimes Dad touched her in ways that didn't feel right.

"I don't know why," she whispered, eyes fixed on her hands. "But I don't like it. It feels… wrong. But I think I must have done something bad to make it happen."

Papa's breath caught, and he swallowed hard, fighting the storm rising inside him. His training, his years as an officer, all kicked in, but so did his heart, breaking for the little girl in his arms.

"Maddie," he said firmly but gently, lifting her chin so she could see the truth in his eyes. "You did nothing wrong. Nothing. None of this is your fault. Do you understand me?"

Her voice was small. "But I make him mad…"

"No," Papa interrupted softly but firmly. "Grown-ups are responsible for their own choices. You are a child. And none of this; not the yelling, not the hurting, not the touching is ever, ever your fault."

Tears streamed down Maddie's cheeks, but this time they felt different. Lighter. As if each one carried a piece of the secret she had held onto for too long. Papa held her close, careful to avoid the sore spot on her back, and let her cry.

When the sobs finally slowed, Maddie's head rested against his chest, her heartbeat steadying with his. The tree lights twinkled softly beside them, and the first hints of dawn crept over the horizon.

Papa brushed a strand of hair from her face. "I'm so proud of you," he whispered. "And I'm going to make sure you're safe, Maddie. I promise you that."

And for the first time in a long time, Maddie believed she would be safe.

Chapter Thirty-Two

The first pale streaks of Christmas morning light crept through the picture window, glinting softly off the snow outside. The Ryder house stirred slowly awake, the faint rustle of wrapping paper, the smell of coffee brewing, and the magical stillness that always seemed to hang in the air on December 25th.

Maddie sat curled in Papa's lap by the tree, Jane tucked securely against her chest. She felt lighter, still tender from what she had shared, but not alone anymore. Papa's promise echoed quietly in her heart: I'm going to make sure you're safe.

Upstairs, footsteps creaked as Mom stirred, and soon Wyatt came clattering down the stairs in his pajamas, his face bright with excitement. "It's Christmas! It's Christmas!" he shouted, sliding to the tree and shaking a box with his name on it.

Papa smiled softly but his mind was elsewhere. As the kids dove into the magic of the morning, tearing paper and squealing over new toys, Papa quietly slipped into the kitchen where Mom was pouring coffee.

"Can we talk?" he asked gently.

The look on his face told her everything. Her hand trembled slightly as she set the mug down. "What's wrong?"

Papa took a deep breath, steadying himself. "Maddie told me some things this morning," he said softly. "Things about... about what's been happening when I'm not here."

Mom's eyes widened, fear flashing in them. "What kind of things?"

Papa's voice remained calm and deliberate, but each word landed like a hammer blow. He told her about the bruises. About the beatings. About the screaming nights. And then, with a heavy heart, he told her about the other part, the part that made his voice falter and Mom's knees nearly buckle.

"She said… he's touched her. In ways that made her feel wrong. That she didn't understand, but she knew weren't okay."

For a long moment, the world seemed to stop. Mom's face went pale, her hands gripping the edge of the counter as if the ground had shifted beneath her. "No…" she whispered, tears spilling down her cheeks. "No… not my baby…"

Papa reached for her hand. "It's not her fault," he said firmly. "None of it is. I told her that. And we're going to protect her. Both of them."

Mom's shoulders shook with quiet sobs. "Their childhood…" she choked out. "It's being stolen from them."

"I know," Papa said softly. "But it's not too late to give them safety, and joy again. That starts now."

They stood together in the kitchen, the weight of truth pressing heavy around them. But there was also a resolve. A shared, unspoken promise to do whatever it took to protect those children.

When they returned to the living room, they tucked their sorrow away behind soft smiles and warm hugs. Today was Christmas, and the children deserved its magic. Papa positioned himself carefully throughout the day, always between the kids and their father, watchful and steady. His presence alone was enough to keep the man subdued, sitting quietly and nursing his beer at the edge of the room.

The day unfolded with laughter and light. Maddie and Wyatt played with their new toys, read from the books they'd unwrapped, and danced around the living room in their pajamas. The smell of cinnamon rolls filled the house, and Mom, though her eyes still shimmered with sadness, laughed as they tried on their new winter hats and showed off their stocking stuffers.

But the most magical moment came after the gifts had been opened and the paper swept away. Papa stood by the tree with an envelope in his hands, his eyes twinkling.

"I have one more surprise," he said, handing it to Mom.

She opened it, her hands trembling, and gasped softly. Inside were plane tickets, park passes, and hotel reservations. "Papa… is this…?"

Papa smiled. "It's a trip for all of you and me to Walt Disney World this April break."

Maddie's eyes grew wide. "Disney World?!" she squealed, nearly dropping Jane in her excitement.

"Yes, sweetheart," Papa chuckled. "We're going to see Cinderella's castle, and you'll get to meet Ariel."

"Really?!" Wyatt shouted, bouncing on his heels. "We're really going?!"

"You are," Papa said, his smile deepening. "The happiest place on Earth where kids should get to be kids."

Maddie threw her arms around him, tears of pure joy streaming down her face. "Thank you, Papa! Thank you, thank you!"

For a moment, the darkness of the past weeks faded, replaced by laughter, hugs, and dreams of castles and fireworks. Maddie pressed her cheek against Papa's shoulder and whispered, "I can't wait."

"I know, little mermaid," he murmured back. "And this time, you'll get to feel nothing but safe and happy. I promise."

And though the shadows of the present still lingered at the edges of the room, the light of that promise, and the magic of that Christmas shone brighter than ever.

Chapter Thirty-Three

When school started back up, Maddie practically *floated* through the front doors. She couldn't wait to tell Breanna, her best friend.

The two of them found their usual spot in the hallway near the coat hooks before the first bell rang. "Guess what?" Maddie blurted out, barely able to contain herself.

"What?" Breanna asked, tilting her head.

"I'm going to Disney World!"

Breanna's eyes widened. "No way!"

"Yes way!" Maddie grinned so hard her cheeks hurt. "I'm going to meet Ariel. I already know what I'm going to say to her. I'm going to thank her for bringing magic into my life."

Breanna giggled and clapped her hands. "You should tell her you want to be a mermaid too!"

"I will," Maddie said with a firm nod. "She wants to be where the people are... but *I* want to be where the mermaids are."

They both burst out laughing, imagining themselves swimming under the sea with Ariel and Flounder, their hair floating like seaweed.

Jake wandered over then, backpack slung over one shoulder. "What's so funny?"

"Maddie's going to Disney World," Breanna said, practically bouncing.

Jake's face lit up. "That's awesome! You're gonna meet Mickey and Goofy and everyone."

Maddie's cheeks flushed under his smile. It was a fluttery feeling she didn't fully understand yet, but it made her happy.

"We're going to make a list of all the things she's going to say to Ariel," Breanna added, looking between them.

Jake chuckled. "You're gonna need a long list. That park's huge."

The first bell rang overhead, echoing down the hallway as kids started hurrying to their classrooms. Jake shifted his backpack and gave Maddie a little wave. "See you in class," he said before heading down the hall to where his friends were waiting.

Breanna smirked. "He likes you," she teased.

Maddie rolled her eyes, but the corners of her mouth gave her away. "No, he doesn't."

Breanna gave her a playful bump. "Uh-huh. Sure he doesn't."

As they turned toward their classroom, Maddie tugged at the sleeve of her sweater, making sure it was pulled all the way down. The fabric brushed against her upper arm, sending a dull ache through the fading bruises beneath. She kept her arm pressed close to her side, hoping no one would notice.

But Breanna had always been observant.

"Maddie... what's that?" she asked softly, her hand gently brushing against the fabric near Maddie's elbow.

Maddie froze. The edge of her sleeve had ridden up just enough to reveal a faint line of yellow and purple bruises dotting her arm, silent evidence of a night she didn't want to think about.

"I…" Maddie swallowed hard, her eyes falling to the floor. "I made my dad mad."

The joy in Breanna's face dimmed, replaced with a soft, quiet worry. She didn't ask more. She didn't have to. Her eyes said everything.

And in that moment, Maddie gained something she didn't expect. Breanna became another person who held Maddie's secret, just like Wyatt, Jane, and the walls of that old house.

The bell rang a second time, breaking the moment. Breanna reached out and gave her hand a gentle squeeze before they walked the last few steps to class together. "I can't wait to hear every single thing about Ariel when you get back," she whispered with a smile.

Maddie nodded, clutching her books tight against her chest. The world outside her home was growing, she had a *circle* of friends who saw her, even if they didn't see everything.

Later that morning, Maddie sat at her desk. The chalk squeaked softly on the blackboard as Mrs. Parker explained a math problem, but the numbers blurred into nothing. Her mind drifted elsewhere, warm and bright.

In her imagination, she wasn't in her classroom anymore. She was standing in front of Cinderella Castle, the Florida sun on her face. She could hear music on Main Street, smell popcorn and sugar in the air. She wore her mermaid dress, the one she'd been saving, and held Jane tight in her hands.

Ariel appeared in front of her, sitting on her seashell throne. "Hi, Maddie," she said with that perfect, warm smile. "I've been waiting for you."

Maddie's voice came out small in her daydream. "I wanted to say thank you… for bringing magic into my life."

Ariel leaned forward. "The magic's been inside you all along, guppy. You just have to believe it."

And just like that, Maddie imagined the two of them diving beneath the water, swimming with fish and starfish swirling around them like glitter. Everything was easy and free.

"Miss Ryder," Mrs. Parker's voice snapped her gently back into reality. Maddie blinked and straightened up fast, cheeks warm. A few kids giggled softly.

"Would you like to share the answer to number five?" Mrs. Parker asked with a kind smile.

Maddie scrambled, flipping through her paper. "Uh… seven?"

Mrs. Parker smiled knowingly. "Close. Let's walk through it together."

As the class continued, Maddie's heart stayed halfway between the chalkboard and Neverland. Even though life at home wasn't safe, she carried the spark of something bright with her, a hope no one could take away.

And from my quiet spot in her backpack, I could feel it, too.

Her dreams were like little embers… glowing, stubborn, keeping the darkness at bay.

Chapter Thirty-Four

By the time April rolled around, the snow had melted from the Vermont mountains, leaving behind damp earth and the first buds of spring. But inside the Ryder house, the air still felt heavy. Since that Christmas morning when Papa had learned the truth, many nights had been hard, nights when shouting rattled the walls, doors slammed, and fear pressed against every corner of Maddie's small world.

But something else had changed too. Mom had made a decision. A quiet, steady, unwavering decision.

She was leaving him.

It hadn't been easy. There had been tears, long talks behind closed doors with Papa, and visits to lawyers. But she knew now what she hadn't let herself believe before: her children deserved to grow up safe. And she was determined to give them that.

The plan was set. While Maddie, Wyatt, Mom, and Papa were in Florida for their Disney trip, Dad would move out. By the time they came home, he would be gone.

And so, one bright April morning, they packed their bags into Papa's car and drove toward the airport, toward sunshine, magic, and a brand-new beginning.

For a whole week, Maddie and her family lived inside the wonder of Walt Disney World.

Every morning, they boarded the ferry from their cozy campsite at Fort Wilderness, the cool breeze on their faces as Cinderella Castle came into view across the lagoon. The air smelled sweet, a mix of popcorn, ice cream, and warm pavement, and the sounds of laughter and music wrapped around them like a blanket.

The magic felt endless. Maddie met Mickey, Minnie, Donald, and Goofy, each hug reminding her what joy was supposed to feel like. She floated through "it's a small world" wide-eyed, spun in dizzy circles on the Teacups, and soared with Dumbo high above Fantasyland.

But nothing compared to meeting Ariel.

The line wound through rock walls shaped like an undersea grotto. When Maddie finally saw Ariel sitting on her seashell throne, her heart nearly leapt out of her chest. She clutched Jane tightly, wearing the mermaid dress her mom had bought just for this trip.

Ariel's smile was warm and real. "Hi there, guppy," she said, reaching out to Maddie. "I love your dress!"

Maddie blushed and whispered, "I wanted to look just like you."

Ariel knelt to her level, her voice soft and kind. "I think you're even more magical than me."

They hugged, and for that moment, Maddie felt like she'd stepped out of her world and into Ariel's.

The family spent their days exploring Fantasy land, flying over London on Peter Pan's Flight, spinning on

Dumbo, and clutching each other tight through Snow White's Scary Adventures. Maddie giggled at the end, proud of how brave she'd been.

One day, they rode the monorail over to Epcot, where Maddie's imagination soared. She and Wyatt shared pastries in the France Pavilion, walked through the United Kingdom, and tilted their heads back in awe beneath the silver dome of Spaceship Earth. Papa pointed out all the little details that made Epcot special, while Maddie just loved how big the world suddenly felt.

The week went by in a blur of laughter, colors, fun music and sunlit afternoons. And then came the most unforgettable night of all.

They stood together in front of Cinderella Castle as the fireworks exploded above them. Reds, blues, golds, and pinks filled the night sky. Maddie tilted her head back, eyes wide, completely mesmerized by the beauty. For the first time in a long time, there was no fear in her chest, only light.

Her mom knelt down and wrapped an arm around her shoulders, holding her close. Papa smiled, his eyes reflecting the fireworks as they bloomed across the sky.

Later, on the ferry ride back to Fort Wilderness, Maddie leaned against her mom, eyelids heavy with happy exhaustion. Her legs ached from walking, her cheeks were warm from the Florida sun, and her heart was full.

As the ferry cut quietly across the water, Maddie looked up at the night sky. And there, just between the stars and the moon, she saw her. A tiny glimmer of light, dancing and twinkling, with a dusting of magic trailing behind.

"Tinker Bell," she whispered sleepily. She could almost see Neverland floating in the night sky.

She closed her eyes, clutching Jane gently, and smiled.

For the first time, Maddie felt like she belonged somewhere safe and magical. She didn't know what waited for her at home, but she knew something had changed inside her. The magic of that week wasn't just in the parks, it was in her heart now.

And no one could take that away.

When they returned home days later, something felt different the moment they stepped inside. The house was quieter. Lighter. The air didn't feel heavy anymore.

He was gone.

His things were missing. The beer cans, the smoke-stained chair, the fire hydrant astray, the anger that had clung to the corners of the house. All gone.

Maddie stood in the living room, Jane tucked under her arm, and breathed deeply. For the first time, the house felt like a home.

"Do you feel it?" Mom asked quietly, coming to stand beside her.

Maddie nodded. "It feels… calm."

Mom knelt and wrapped her in a hug. "That's how it's going to stay."

Papa put an arm around both of them, his eyes warm. "This is a new chapter," he said. "A better one."

And though Maddie knew there would still be hard days ahead, she also knew this: the worst was behind them. The magic she had felt in Disney, the joy, the wonder, the safety wasn't just in Florida. It was here now, too. It lived in her home, in her family, and deep within her heart.

The trip had changed everything. And from that day forward, life would never be the same again.

Chapter Thirty-Five

My place never changed.
Even as posters replaced picture books on the walls,
and the music in Maddie's room grew louder and bolder,
my spot was always on her bed. I'd sit against her
pillow, right where I'd been since the beginning. A quiet,
constant presence in a world that had changed a
thousand times around us.

I watched the little girl I'd once protected grow into a
young woman. Gone were the pigtails and princess
dresses, replaced by ripped jeans, oversized hoodies,
and the quiet confidence that only comes from surviving
something most people never see. Maddie had
changed, and so had her world.

When she turned thirteen, Maddie made one of the
bravest choices of her life. For years, court orders had
forced her to visit her father. Each trip carried the
familiar weight of fear. The unthinkable had happened in
that house more than once, and though she never
spoke of all of it out loud, I felt it every time she held me
a little tighter before and after those visits.

But at thirteen, Maddie found her voice. She told the
court she did not feel safe, and this time, people
listened. She no longer had to go back.

Though they were not entirely free, because trauma
lingers even after the doors are closed, it was no longer
part of their everyday lives. Maddie could breathe again.
She could laugh without constantly looking over her
shoulder.

Wyatt, older and carrying his own wounds in quieter
ways, still chose to see their dad. Everyone copes

differently, and I understood this wasn't about right or wrong, just different paths to survival.

The years rolled forward like a tide. Maddie became a teenager with dreams bigger than the pain that once defined her. She decorated her room, planned her future, and clung to the few constants she trusted. Her brother, her mom, her Papa, and me.

In their early twenties, the call came. Their father was gone. Blood infections. Cirrhosis of the liver. Years of destruction had finally caught up to him.

Maddie sat quietly that day, holding me in her lap. Her face wasn't one of shock, but of something deeper. A mixture of relief, sorrow, and a quiet ache for the father she never truly had. She didn't cry for the man he became. She cried for the little girl who had needed him to be someone he never was.

Her mother, determined to keep healing moving forward, made sure both Maddie and Wyatt got into therapy. Therapy gave them words for their pain and the tools to shape their futures without it defining who they were.

I watched her grow stronger. She still carried the weight of the past, but it no longer crushed her. It became a part of her story but not the whole of it.

And even as the years pulled her further from those dark nights, every evening, without fail, Maddie still reached for me. Her room changed. She changed. But my spot on her bed never did.

Because some things, the ones that carried us through, stay.

And somewhere between the healing and the growing, Maddie found something more. She discovered a calling. A fire inside her to make sure no child ever felt as alone as she once did. She spoke louder now. She fought for others. She became the person she had needed all along.

I knew then, even before the nursery, that this story wasn't ending.
It was beginning again. This time with love, with strength, and with her.

Chapter Thirty-Six

From my spot on the nursery chair, I could see everything. The soft morning light filtered through pale curtains, casting a golden glow over the room. The gentle scent of baby lotion hung in the air, and the faint hum of a lullaby mobile spun lazily above the crib.

The chair was cushioned and cozy, draped with a knitted blanket in shades of soft pink and cream. It was the perfect place to sit and watch, a quiet perch from which I could take in the world Maddie had built.

This nursery was different from any room I'd ever known. There were no cracks in the walls, no shadows hiding behind closed doors. There was warmth here, real warmth, and peace. And for the first time in decades, I knew that this tiny soul who would soon call this nursery home would grow up knowing only love.

It had been many years since Maddie was that scared little girl who clutched me on the stairs while the world below her crumbled. After the divorce, life had changed slowly at first, cautiously like a spring thaw. There were still court-ordered visits with her father. Those days were hard. Each goodbye left her quiet and withdrawn. But something inside Maddie had shifted on that Disney trip. She had learned that safety and joy were possible, and she refused to settle for anything less.

By the time she turned thirteen, Maddie made a choice, one of the most powerful of her life. She stopped going back. She had a voice now, and she used it. She told the courts she was done, that she deserved peace. And they listened.

From that point on, Maddie's life took a new direction. She poured herself into school, into learning, into dreaming of a future where no child would ever feel as small or as scared as she once had. Somewhere along the way, a dream took root, to become a teacher, not just to educate but to protect.

And she did. Maddie grew into a fierce advocate for children. She taught them letters and numbers, yes; but she also taught them that they mattered. That they were safe. That they were loved. And when she saw signs of hurt or fear, she acted. Dozens of children found their way out of unsafe homes because Maddie spoke up. Because she remembered. Because she knew.

And now… this was her next chapter.

I glanced around the nursery again, my heart swelling with something that felt very much like pride. "This time," I whispered to the quiet room, "your baby will know nothing but love."

A soft sound behind me made me turn, and there, gathered together once again, were familiar faces I hadn't seen in years.

"Rabberta!" I gasped.

The pink bunny, still with her floppy ears and slightly crooked googly eyes, hopped clumsily toward me from the corner shelf. Her fur was a little more worn than I remembered, but her spirit was the same. "Jane!" she exclaimed, wrapping her soft arms around me. "Oh, how I've missed you."

"And me!" came a gentle voice from the doll crib. Trisha, ever calm and kind, sat propped against a tiny pillow, her painted eyes still full of warmth. "It's been far too long."

My fabric heart swelled. "It's good to see you both," I said, and it truly was. They had been my companions through nights of fear and days of imagination. Protectors, just like me. And now, here we were again, reunited not in sorrow, but in hope.

"This little one," Rabberta said, glancing toward the crib with a smile, "will grow up surrounded by love. That's our job now."

"And we're ready," Trisha added softly. "We've done this before, but this time, we'll get to see the happy ending."

I looked toward the door, where I could hear Maddie's soft footsteps approaching, not the tiny hurried steps of a frightened girl, but the steady, confident stride of a woman who had rebuilt her life piece by piece.

And I knew, deep within the stitches and seams of my being, that this story wasn't just hers anymore. It was about every child she would protect, every life she would touch, and now, about a new life about to begin.

This time, there would be lullabies without fear. Laughter without tension. A childhood without shadows.

And the Night Council, reunited at last and watching from the nursery chair, would stand guard over it all.

Author's Note

This story is based on true events.

For much of my life, I carried a secret, one stitched into my childhood like the seams of Jane herself. The pain, the fear, the nights filled with shouting and silence, the confusion of being hurt by someone who was supposed to protect me... all of it was real. And for a long time, it defined me.

But I made a choice.

I chose to survive.
I chose to rise.
I chose to build a life that was bigger and brighter than the darkness I was born into.

This story isn't about tragedy, it's about transformation. It's about a little girl who found safety in the arms of a beloved doll, strength in the love of her grandfather and family, and courage in the belief that her story didn't have to end in pain. It's about reclaiming a childhood that was stolen and rewriting it with healing, hope, and purpose.

Today, I work to help children like Maddie. Children who are living through their own storms, who feel invisible, not heard, forgotten, or afraid. Through my own trauma, I've found my mission: to protect, to advocate, and to help guide them toward safety and freedom.

If you see yourself in Maddie's story, please know this: you are not alone. You never were. And your story does not end with what was done to you. It is possible to heal. It is possible to build a life full of love and laughter and purpose, even after everything.

I wrote this book not just to share my truth, but to reach the hearts of those still searching for theirs. If even one person feels seen, less alone, or more hopeful after reading these pages, then every painful memory I've revisited here will have been worth it.

From one survivor to another:
You are stronger than you think.
You are worthy of safety, of love, and of joy.
And your story isn't over yet.

— Shannon

www.ingramcontent.com/pod-product-compliance
Lightning Source LLC
LaVergne TN
LVHW052028080426
835513LV00018B/2225